You are enough!

Nita

*To my Mother.*
*For your strength, your love of family and all the lessons you*
*continue to teach me*

*Introduction*

I have written the beginning of this book a million times in my mind.

These stories and lines would whirl around in my head each time I thought about putting pen to paper. One of these lines is the perfect description of me:

**I am no one special.**

I'm not trying to degrade myself or downplay my place in the hearts of those I'm close to. It's more to put myself in every woman's shoes.

I don't have a magic formula. I definitely didn't have all the answers, nor do I now.

What I can give you is my experiences, my strength, and my hope.

In one of my first sessions with my attorney during my second divorce, I told her my tale. Her next words were, "You're going to need a therapist in order to be my client." I found this lovely, professional Jewish woman by starting with "W" under attorney in the yellow pages of the new city I moved to during this divorce. (I always hated the lazy marketing practice of starting your business with an "A" so people would call you first.) When she told me to get a therapist during our first meeting, I was shocked, but soon realized she was more than an attorney, she was a woman who cared about other women's mental health. She could do all the legal stuff to help but she needed my mind to be whole as well.

I made an appointment with her recommendation, thinking in my professional mind, "OK, let's get this over so we can move forward."

I was clear with the therapist that I would tell her my story and then if she could just give me the top five things I could do to get my head straight, that would be great.

Are you smiling when you read this? You should be. Obviously, there is no magic formula. There is no list.

Our experiences make us who we are, and our shared experiences tell us we aren't alone in our thoughts.

I spent 28 years raising children in my home. The oldest of my eight children is 15 years older than the baby. If you did the math, you're thinking, wait, 15 years apart and the last one leaving at 18 equals 31? Did she kick the last one out in middle school? Nope!

God placed some of these children in my life not at birth, but during some pretty rough times in their life.

I spent 32 years working with the same company, moving from an independent contractor to a Vice President of a sales force.

My career started seven years after I became a mother for the first time. My experiences with both motherhood and my career go hand in hand.

Mine is not a fairytale story of meeting my Prince Charming on the first go around and riding off into the sunset.

My story is real. My story is written from my experiences and the lessons I have learned.

Someone asked me if I was embellishing or changing the names of the people in my story.

First, no need to embellish. It's quite a story.

Second, my story isn't about someone doing something TO me. My story is about how I moved forward through what life threw at me. In some cases, not very gracefully. It's about standing tall when at times I really wanted to throw in the towel.

My story is about hope.

I am no one special.

I am a daughter, a mother, a sister, a wife (and ex-wife), a grandmother, a woman in leadership, a friend, and a mentor to many.

This story comes from my heart. The only way for me to write from my heart is to actually write...with a pen. The original manuscript of my story was written in long hand. Yep, I wrote, in cursive, this entire book. To type something so personal felt cold and surface-level.

Writing my story for you with pen in hand felt like a hug we could share. And Lord knows as professional women who are also raising our beautiful kiddos, we all need a lot of hugs.

At one point in writing the chapter on Inner Strength I had an anxiety attack. I don't mean just a little anxiety; I mean the whole deal! Heart palpitations, sweaty palms, and the feeling of wanting to throw up.

"How ridiculous!" I told myself. "I know how it all ends!"

Not ridiculous at all. Life is stressful. You may know how things turn out but reliving it can bring all those emotions right back out again.

Compare it to rewatching the Wonder Woman movie. You know she's going to survive; you know good beats evil but damn if I'm not on the edge of my seat when she's kicking evil's ass every time I watch it.

It is not my intention to blame or hurt anyone in the telling of my story. If for some reason I have then please know that from my heart I am sorry.

I am no one special. I am a farmer's daughter with no college degree who worked hard and fought hard. I always tried to err on the side that would benefit others. I am definitely not perfect. I am someone who thanks God every day for my life. Even those days when finding something to be grateful for is difficult.

I am every professional woman who is also a mother.

I hope you will take time after every chapter to write down your reflections on the pages in the back of this book. Writing down my thoughts, whether personal journaling or taking the best notes in a meeting, has been a lifesaver for me. Many times, I have gone back to my journals for inspiration. I cannot count the times I have been asked for my meeting notes or heard from team members, "You're going to recap and send your notes to me, right?"

Rereading your own thoughts and stories during difficult times we face, as professional women who are also mothers, can provide perspective and motivation.

Thank you for taking this Walk With Me.

# CHAPTER 1

## *Tenacity*

I t feels right to start my story with this word: tenacity.

I can't say I knew what it meant when someone told me I had this trait. I had to ask her what that meant.

She told me that I had the ability to keep standing no matter what life threw at me.

I stood there for a moment thinking about that and replied, "I didn't really have a choice."

You see, through three marriages and raising eight children along with a highly demanding career, I could not be the one to fall. People depended on me to stand tall and not fall.

But fall I did. It wasn't the falling that led to my tenacity, it was my ability to get back up.

Time and time again life will knock you on your ass. Sometimes so hard that it seems you will never get back up. Even though laying there sometimes feels better. I mean, I'm laying here anyway, why not relax for a minute! You know the moments when you are flat on your back and looking up at the clouds trying to make animals out of them or staring at the stars searching for the big dipper.... And maybe while you were down there some magic Genie would come over and grant you three wishes.... We all know that's not going to happen but it's a nice break from reality before you get back up.

And get back up you will, just as I did. You must remember during those knock-you-on-your-ass moments that you aren't alone. Sometimes all you can do to help yourself is reach up and grab ahold of someone's hand for their support and strength. Those people are out there. You may not even know who they are until you need that hand. But they are out there!

I hope you noticed that I used the word "fall" instead of "fail." I don't believe we fail; I believe we learn from every fall. Each fall we take has a lesson.

Sometimes it takes years to see the lesson, but trust me, you will.

And sometimes the lesson is immediate. Like the time I literally fell going into a store. My husband was holding my hand and I was wearing the coolest boots with a spiky heel... in December. The second my man let go of my hand, down I went.

Immediate lesson learned: don't let go of your man when you are wearing spiky-heeled boots in December!

Lessons of other falls took longer to figure out.

As I look back at my story of two failed marriages, raising eight children and a 32-year career I am continually amazed at how my life turned out.

When people ask, "How did you do it?" I truly have no answer. Like most women, I just did it.

The lessons of those long-ago falls are the answer. I found the key.

The key was tenacity! I never gave up...... until I had to.

In my early 20's I thought men were like home improvement projects, and that was par for the course in a marriage. Find one with some good structure and then do a little personality remodel and "TADA!," perfect husband. I learned the hard way that this is not the case.

What you see during the "honeymoon" of your first dates is not what you are getting, ladies. I'm not implying that you can't grow and learn with the right partner as I have with #3. I'm saying if you see signs of abuse or addiction, you can't remodel them like you would your bathroom.

I'll admit, even after Marriage #1, I hadn't learned my lesson. It was Marriage #2 that it finally got through to me.

While we were dating, he admitted to an alcohol problem. #1 had an alcohol problem that he never admitted to, so I thought, "Ok, apparently, I am attracted to men that don't drink well."

I mean, these guys are fun! They are always the life of the party and everyone's best friend! Who doesn't fall for them?

Because #2 admitted the problem, I believed I was making a better choice. He went through his first treatment program while we were dating - no red flag there. He was raising his three kids as a single Dad and owned his own business. I jumped right in! I can help this man change. After all, he wanted to!

His fourth treatment program was eight years later – after we separated.

It would take years in therapy to learn how to deal with my attraction to wounded men. At the end of one therapy session, my therapist looked at me and said, "You may still be attracted to these types of men, but you won't give them your phone number." This still makes me laugh years later!

It's important for me to say that the men I married are the father of my children. Each had great qualities that I see in our children, and I am grateful for that. I try to be careful to share the good stories with my children about their fathers. They know that they are part of this person and if all I told them were the negatives then I believed that is how they would see themselves.

#2 died when the youngest of our six was 15. He died homeless, still battling his addiction.

These are the falls I had to give up on. Was it really giving up if I decided to make a different life for my children?

What I will never give up on are my children. I can't say that I have a great relationship with all eight of these wonderful adults, but I hope I showed them a different way to live - without addiction.

I believe that God put all eight of these children in my life for a reason. It was my primary job to show them a better path, or at the very least, a different one than they saw in their earlier lives.

Did I succeed? That's a tough question and one I will address in a later chapter.

I must say that my 32-year career never gave me the huge life challenges my personal life did.

Once I walked into my office, I knew I had complete control of what success or "falls" I would have that day. Once I got home, I never knew what I would be facing.

When I started my career in the late 80's, I was a single mom working three jobs to make ends meet.

During the day, I managed an office for a dentist who had been in practice for over 40 years. He was a kind but direct man who wanted to turn me into his assistant so that his wife could reduce her time in the office.

It only took me two disgusting mouth surgeries to know that this was not a path I would take. I was happy just managing his office and calendar.

In the evenings I would either waitress or bartend at a local dinner house. The dinner house was owned by the most-recent past Chief of Police who was also a gentle and kind man. He didn't like that I had to work in the evenings and tried to give me the best shifts to make the most tips. I begged him to let me bartend and he finally gave in and let me bartend on the slow nights so I could learn how to run the bar.

I was so fortunate to have a day care provider who was flexible in hours as well as forgiving if I couldn't afford to pay my entire bill each week.

God winked when he had a recruiter for an insurance company stop at the dinner house on his way through town each month. He would always sit in my section, and when he could, ask me about my life. I was, of course, busy but would make him laugh with stories of my kids or my adventures during my day job.

Over the course of a few months, he would tell me what he did for a living and suggested I take a minute to talk with him further. I didn't pay much attention at first, I just smiled and said maybe when I have some time.

I finally relented when he left me a note on his table with how much they would pay me to sell insurance to farmers and ranchers.

This gentleman offered me a job AND was going to pay me more than all three of my current jobs.

What?!

I don't have a college degree, nor any sales experience - let alone experience in insurance. Why me? What did he see?

He told me he saw someone with the ability to work with all types of people while waitressing and bartending. He saw someone who worked hard and didn't take bullshit.

Well, ok... that *did* sound like me.

I made a leap of faith. Not just in the amazing company I would go on to work for over the course of 32 years, but also in myself.

In the late 80's the insurance industry was a man's world. The agency I joined was not only all men, but older white men who all spoke the same language, laughed at the same jokes, and had worked together for years.

As a 25-year-old uneducated, outspoken woman with no experience, I felt intimidated and out of my element. Walking into that first sales meeting, I made a decision: I was going to give this one year. I called it my "in the meantime" job—I was just going to do this in the meantime while I find another option.

This group of men were welcoming and kind—at the time. I remember thinking I will never know as much as they do.

One man stood out as the leader. When he spoke, everyone listened and agreed without question. If he was upset about something they would all become upset. If he was happy well then, they were as well. He was a kind and gentle man who at first seemed unapproachable.

But I had questions. Dare I ask? Would they think I was just a stupid girl? Would they laugh at me behind my back, or worse, the minute I asked?

This was swirling around my mind as I raised my hand, "I have a question."

Years later a peer would tell me that the meeting didn't really get interesting until I raised my hand.

I learned the hard way what could happen if you didn't ask questions. No question is too big or too small when you are starting a new position.

I took a job years earlier in a bank. Way before automated systems and computers. Everything was done manually and again I was hired with no experience other than good interview skills. I was afraid to ask questions in fear that I would appear unworthy of the job. I struggled every day to figure out routine transactions or office procedures. This job did not last long. With self-evaluation, I realized that had I just asked for the information I needed to accomplish my tasks, my time there would have gone much smoother. I vowed to not let that happen again.

The kind and gentle soul from that first meeting didn't make me feel lesser than because I had questions. He told me that day that the key to success was to give myself permission to ask questions. It's the only way to learn and better serve your clients.

I'm sure he regretted this statement after my 500th question but you would never have known. He was a true leader. Not just in his sales production, but in his ability to lead people. I learned a great deal about leadership from him.

The year I broke his records on the sales team felt awkward to me. How would he feel about me now? Would he still answer my questions or keep his secrets to himself so he could continue to be #1?

That was not the case. He walked right up to me in that crowded room and hugged me. He told me how proud he was of me and how he had believed in me from the first time he met me.

Wow! All this time I thought I annoyed him and perhaps he put up with me because he was just a really nice guy. My heart soared at his words. Before going into that room, I thought I had a lucky year. When I left, I felt like I had the world by the tail!

In all my years of leadership, I remembered that feeling. I made it a point to try to help others feel the same way about their achievements.

Lessons I learned about leadership from this man:

Be kind always

Be gracious

Listen like you mean it

You're never too good not to learn

Your words are everything, use them wisely

Praise often

Around the time I made the decision that this job was just "in the meantime," God gave me an AHA moment.

As I mentioned, I was a single mom when I started with the company. I had a six-year-old and a four-year-old. My four-year-old was severely asthmatic with many hospital stays. He needed daily breathing treatments to keep his lungs clear and working properly. We lived in a single wide trailer in a mobile home park.

Wait, that makes it sound better than it was. The term "trailer park" and all the negative jokes about trailer parks is closer. It was situated close to downtown so there were rules about junk in the yard, thank goodness. However, the rental trailers themselves left a lot to be desired. It was so terrible that I refused to have my parents over when they came to town. It was the best I could do at that time.

The funny thing is that it was a place I finally felt safe. Safe from the unknown of an alcoholic spouse who you had to tiptoe around. The kind of safe where you can take a deep breath every time you walk through the front door. I had a sense of freedom in that crappy single wide trailer that I wasn't relying on another person for a roof over our head and food on the table.

One morning, not long after I made the declaration that I would just do this job for a year, I woke up to sounds of laughter from my babies. I was happy to hear that my four-year-old was feeling better and that his big sister was taking care of him so I could sleep in. I jumped out of bed ready to join them in their giggles and stopped dead in my tracks at the bedroom door.

It was the middle of winter. There was a snowdrift in the hallway from the storm the night before. It was freezing cold in the house and there was a snowdrift inside my home!

My babies thought this was the best day ever. They could play in the snow inside the house. They couldn't understand why I was crying, not joining in on their fun.

At that moment I realized I could do better. I would do better! I would take this "in the meantime" job and give it everything I had to give them a better life. A life without snow in the hallway.

One of my most recognizable traits was born on one of the hardest days of my life. Tenacity.

* * *

*Take a moment to reflect and write down your thoughts. Note pages are available in the back of the book.*

CHAPTER 2

*Choices & Consequences*

H ave you ever wondered what your life would be like if you took the "other" path?

When you are faced with those life changing choices, how do you determine the right one?

As I look back at some of these choices I made, I can see how truly life changing they were, not only for myself, but for my family and those around me.

For most choices, the consequences turned out well but certainly not all. Of course, you can't know that at the time. The anxiety of these moments can cause you to second guess yourself. Anxiety can literally come across as a physical illness with heart palpitation, nausea, and cold sweats. Some of these moments of anxiety are definitely not a highlight in my life.

The word "consequence" has always had a negative sound. Remember the game, Truth or Consequence, where you and your friends would stay up all night asking secret questions and if you didn't answer or if you didn't tell the truth you had to face the consequences? Or your parents telling you that you would face the consequences of your actions? Every choice you make, every path you choose, has consequences. I choose to use this word more as an equal sign to making difficult choices – here, it has a neutral connotation.

This choice, this path, EQUALS the consequence.

Determining the right path is not easy - especially as a mother. Every decision, every path you choose changes the outcome of your children's lives. The responsibility of this can be overwhelming and, for me, some of the scariest moments in my life.

What if I choose the wrong path? It is better to stay in the current situation and just see how it plays out? It can be easier to stay with what you know. Choices are uncomfortable. Change is uncomfortable.

Making the choice to be uncomfortable changed my life. With these choices, I was able to see a whole new perspective. I could no longer just blaze through everyday knowing what was going to happen. I had to slow down, sometimes stop altogether and really think about the next steps on this new path, this new choice.

I was excited and afraid at the same time!

Remember those recognizable traits in the last chapter? How are these traits born during the hardest times in your life?

Bravery is born from fear!

I have had many people tell me that I am brave.

Brave for leaving an abusive relationship.

Brave for moving my family away from everything they knew.

Brave for being a woman in a man's world.

I can tell you for certain that I didn't feel brave during these colossal life decisions. I was scared and felt very alone. I alone had the power to say, "Yes, I will take that change" or, "No, I don't think I can do it."

No matter how many times I may write my pros and cons lists, no matter the trusted advice from friends and family—nothing alleviated the responsibility that bore down on me.

First and foremost, I am a mom. Our little blessings don't have the same choices we do. I have often said during sales meetings, "You are the advocate for those that have no say in the decision-making."

As a mother, you are the advocate for your children.

As I look back at my life and the brave choices I made, I realize that so much of who I am and how I make decisions is based on watching my parents.

Let me share a story with you about my mother. The bravest woman I will ever know.

I grew up in the same farmhouse where my father spent his summers with his aunt and uncle. It was an amazing childhood. We had 50 acres to run and play and farm on. My brothers and I could and did get into endless adventures, never leaving our farm.

My parents were high school sweethearts who married at 18 & 20. Within three years they had three babies. I didn't realize at the time, nor did my brothers, that we were very poor —the kind of poor where your parents stress about putting food on the table.

Even as a single mom, I don't remember that kind of fear. Dinner wasn't always all food groups, but we always had food on the table.

My parents grew our vegetables and we spent summers freezing, canning, and pickling everything we could.

We have a family joke about guessing what the meat was in the stew or sauce Mom made. After turtle soup, I stopped asking!

My dad worked in a papermill at night and farmed during the day. He was the most adventurous dad in the neighborhood. There was nothing he wouldn't try. The best example of this was the day he waterskied on our pond with a truck pulling him. How he could make us laugh! Wrestling after dinner with all three of us was nightly ritual that drove my mother crazy. "Someone is going to get hurt!" was heard every night.

Well, that someone ended up being Dad. They were headed out for an evening of fun with friends, and we begged Dad to wrestle before they left. Of course, he jumped right in and with giggles, arms and legs of his children all over him.

The next thing we knew Dad was missing a front tooth. One of us hit him with a knee to the mouth and broke a tooth out of his top denture. Oops!

Dad didn't miss a beat. Out the door they went in their finest, Dad looking like a jack-o-lantern saying how much fun he was going to have making up stories about how he lost a tooth.

Our childhood was amazing.

We lost our baby brother not very long ago. He called me to tell me there was nothing more they could do; he just wanted to come home to die. My brother ended the call with, "Thank you for my childhood." It was this time in his life that he talked about the most during his illness. He remained grateful for our childhood experiences until the day he died. I'm sure he is in heaven with our dad today, still sharing some of those amazing memories.

As with most couples, my parents were opposites, think Sandra Dee and Fonzie.

Mom, with her high school diploma, became an advocate for all women. She never backed down from a fight over right and wrong especially when it came to women's rights.

In the late 60s or early 70s Mom became the primary breadwinner in our family. She worked in a paint factory, which was mainly male employees. To tell my mother that a woman couldn't do a man's job were fighting words.

During this time, she went to a well-known clothing store and applied for a credit card. She qualified with her income alone, a significant tribute to her financial wisdom. Imagine, just a few years prior she struggled with how to put food on the table with all three of her babies in diapers. This was a huge step forward.

The store informed her that although she qualified on her own, her husband would have to come in and sign for her. I do believe I saw smoke come out of her ears that day. She walked out of that store, and it took many years for them to win back her business.

Mom was always learning. She started a job as a receptionist at a construction company that builds nuclear power plants. She knew this job would support her family and provide possibilities to learn and advance.

She started night school focusing on accounting because she was always good with numbers. There was a period where I never saw her without a textbook and a pencil in her hand.

As a child, I didn't realize how stressful this was for her, but she was determined to provide a better life for her family. In a short matter of time—at least it seemed quickly to me—she was promoted from receptionist to project accountant. Another position that was filled mostly by men.

She was past her bra burning days but not past standing up for a woman's right to work in any position a man could.

This is when she made a choice that altered her children's lives.

What started out as a conversation with her boss, about women being just as capable or better than a man in her current position, turned into her boss making a statement *almost* as bad as the guy at that clothing store:

"Women can't relocate."

As with most large construction companies, the job is eventually complete, and employees are displaced or relocate within the company. Powerplants can take up to 20 years to complete, so it's not a daily concern when you are working at the site. And while most workers are local, leadership or specialists in areas, such as accounting, do relocate.

Her boss's comment was fighting words to my mother.

She retaliated, "That's not true," and his immediate response was, "Ok, I want you to relocate to Northern Nevada."

Yikes! From upstate New York, where she had lived her whole life, to the wild west!

My adventurous father was all in, and the course of our family's life was changed forever.

I was a senior in high school at the time, and like most teenage girls, extremely emotional. I don't remember throwing a fit, but I am sure that is exactly what happened.

The decision was made. My older brother and I were left in New York, while my parents took my little brother with them.

Stop and think about what turmoil must have been going on in her head. Not only was she leaving everything she had ever known, but she was moving 3,000 miles away from two of her children—who were only 17 and 18 at the time. This was not a time of cell phones. Long distance phone calls were a luxury, and airline tickets were not affordable.

I have no doubt that her bravery was born at this time. I never saw her turmoil. She would never let her children see anything other than poise and confidence.

I stayed with my Grandparents making stupid-teenage-girl decisions. At one point, I thought it made sense to marry my high school boyfriend, even though we had no source of income, or even a general idea how that could work. My thought at that time was I no longer had the home I grew up in, so I'll just make one myself. I only made it four months before deciding I couldn't live without my mother. How I handled the separation from that high school boyfriend is one of my regrets. I worked hard to graduate early and headed out West, telling him I was only going for a visit. Then, I basically just disappeared from his life. Years later, I attempted to reach out to him to apologize. He wouldn't take my call.

My big brother made it almost two years and then he also made the move.

My Uncle and his family followed soon after.

The path she chose impacted so many lives. We can't know what our lives would have been like if she decided to stay in her comfort zone. We *do* know that the consequences of her choice have given us a pretty good life.

She continues to teach us how to manage and live through life's hard choices. Her strength is amazing to me, and I am forever grateful that God chose her to be my mother.

She would relocate with her company three more times during her career. My adventurous father moving along with her each time. My younger brother did end up in Texas with them but the rest of us stayed in Northern Nevada for quite some time.

The West became our home and when she retired, they moved back to Nevada, our family was together once again.

I realized how difficult that first relocation must have been when it was my turn to make the decision to relocate my family for my career.

I believe the choice was easier...at first.

Husband #2 and I had just separated. He was in a treatment center for the fourth time. Five of our six children still lived at home, and I was ready for a change.

When the offer came, the choice to move to Oregon was exciting for all of us. We had vacationed there every summer, so the thought—at first—was we would be on permanent vacation.

Then reality set in.

I would have to go alone to find a place to live. The five children at home were between six and sixteen years old, which meant elementary, middle, and high schools would need to be found. I would have to rent a house not only big enough for all of us, but as a single Mom, close to these new schools, so I could perform well in the job I was hired for.

As with most companies, once you receive the offer, you don't have long to make your decision, move, and get started in your new position. There is no allowance of time just because you are a single mom with five kids, let alone transition your business to the next agent. I had less than a month to make all this happen.

Then, God threw us a curveball.

My 12-year-old son crashed off his skateboard, lacerating his spleen. He was bleeding internally. Due to his severe asthma, they did not want to remove his spleen as it helps with building your immune system—or something like that. I was a wreck!

It was decided he had to stay in the hospital flat on his back to allow his spleen to heal itself. The answer to how long "long" was? "As long as it takes. Estimating two weeks."

I was due to report to my new job in less than ten days.

Even as I write this, I can feel the anxiety of that time. Could I really leave him? Would they delay my starting date to give me extra time to get there? What kind of mother was I to even think about leaving?

The answer to the question, "Can I have more time?" was a solid "No." The agency I was taking over was a complete mess and they needed someone there now. I needed to decide if I wanted the position, or they would have to consider me for *another* position whenever one should be available.

At this time, out of the 90 managers, only one other was a woman, and she was slated to start in her agency the same day I was to start in mine. I knew this type of offer wasn't going to come again anytime soon.

My thoughts went back to my mother's boss saying women can't relocate. Here we are, 16 years later, and the same words are (implicitly) being spoken. Could I let them be right? What is the best choice for my entire family AND for my career, our only means of financial support?

Like so many times in my life, my parents were my sounding board. I think I actually crawled into my father's lap and cried trying to make the right choice.

My son was doing well and being still so he could heal. The doctors assured me he would not need surgery. I made the decision to stay with him as long as I could, then my mother would take over sitting with him at the hospital. When he was released (whenever that would be) he would go home with her.

I left the day before I was to report to my new job. I only had time to pack my clothes and my pillow. The nine-hour drive was awful. I cried most of the way. "I have to be the worst mother in the world" was the constant thought running thought my head. "I am selfish!" "I'm choosing my career over my child!"

Gone were the rational thoughts of how much better this move would make our lives: a fresh start, a bigger town with more opportunities for my children, and a position I worked hard to get.

When I pulled into a hotel in our new city, exhausted, I was ready to turn around and go back the next day.

That's when I found the strength to go on.

As I was checking into the hotel, I reached inside my purse to find an envelope with my name on it in my father's handwriting. I have no idea when he slipped it in there, but it must have been when he was hugging me goodbye earlier that morning.

*Anita,*

*It's times like this in your life when difficult decisions must be made and accounted for not only by others, but more importantly yourself. In the last couple days you have made several of these difficult decisions and I as your father am so proud of you for standing tall and strong while making those decisions. This I am sure is one of the qualities your superiors have seen in you.*

*Love you Nita,*
*Dad*

It's amazing how hearing positive reinforcement and validations can change our attitude so quickly. I had only heard my own negative comments for the past nine hours.

With those words from the man who was my superhero, I stood tall and made a new life for myself and my children.

The path I chose wasn't all rainbows and unicorns. We struggled together and individually.

One of my better decisions during this time was counseling. No stigma about mental health in this family. We needed to learn how to communicate effectively and find tools to deal with these life-altering changes.

Recently, I was discussing the benefits of counseling to one of my adult children as she struggles with communicating with her teenage daughter. While at the time her comments were against the counseling she was "forced" into, I believe that as she grew older, she saw the benefits and it allowed her to seek counseling with no stigma in her adult years.

During the time of our relocation, I sensed the youngest of those at home was really struggling. New home, new school, and his dad was in rough shape. He was struggling in school before the relocation, and this huge change set him back further. I decided to have him repeat first grade to give him a better chance at growth and, of course, got him into counseling.

Every day he would ask me to stay home with him. I would hug and tickle him to lighten the mood and tell him jokingly if Mommy didn't go to work, we would have to live in a box under the bridge and because he was the cutest, he would have to hold a sign asking for food. We would laugh about how big the box would have to be to fit all of us and off to school we would go.

During one of his counseling sessions his therapist asked what scared him the most. He nonchalantly told him he was afraid of having to live in a box. YIKES! Be careful what you joke about to a child!

Effective communication skills are learned, not given, apparently.

Amidst these monumental life decisions, I had a battle between my head, my heart, and my gut. Which one should I listen to?

When I was a little girl, going for a ride to get ice cream with my maternal grandparents was a special treat. What flavor to order was a big decision for a little girl. My grandfather was a quiet man, never really saying more than a grumble if asked a question. He gave me my first lesson on how to know what you really wanted when faced with a tough decision.

"Let's flip a coin," he said.

That seemed logical to my eight-year-old self, so I agreed. He took a quarter out of his pocket and said, "Heads it's chocolate, Tails it's vanilla." And he flipped the coin into the air.

While I anxiously looked over the back seat (this was before law-enforced seat belts) to see if it was heads or tails, he kept the quarter hidden in his hand. He asked me, "When the coin was in the air what were you hoping it land on?"

"Chocolate!" I replied.

"Then there is no reason to see if it's heads or tails. Your gut told you chocolate!"

While we, as mothers and professional women, can't make life-altering decisions this way, I must admit I have secretly used my grandfather's way of checking my gut.

What about those bad decisions or the time we chose the wrong path? Especially when that path ultimately hurts someone you care about?

I have been asked if I would make all the same decisions or choose the same paths I took again—knowing I would end up where I am.

The answer is no.

I wish I could go back and change a couple of those

choices. They still cause me regret and sadness when I think of those who were hurt as a result of my decision.

I know we don't have a crystal ball. I know I didn't make any decisions to intentionally hurt the people I cared for, but I carry the blame and the responsibility, nonetheless.

At times, the regret can become overwhelming. One counselor gave me a tool that I use to ease that overwhelming feeling. She told me that we make decisions based on where we are in our lives at the time of the decision-making. That doesn't mean we would make the same choice today. We learn and grow through our choices and if faced with the same choice today, we may choose differently.

She also helped me see that not all choices are forever. Sometimes, we make choices for today.

I used this as I mentored other women in my professional life. Make the choice and live with it for a day or a week. Does it still feel right? Or are your head, heart and gut still battling? You will be amazed at your power to make tough decisions by trying them on for size.

It's important for me to talk about my faith when discussing choices in my life. I believe in a Higher Power, and for me that is Jesus Christ. I believe he has a plan for all of us. I believe he puts obstacles in our path to build life skills and the character we need for the path he has put us on.

I believe in Thy will be done. Even though I still think *my* will at times.

I believe in the power of prayer. I believe that we go to a better place when our bodies are done here on Earth.

These beliefs have been my one true constant and comfort throughout my entire life.

There were times of struggle in my life where the only place I could find peace was on my knees praying for strength.

I have the luxury of seeing how, up to this point, He has had his hand on my shoulder my whole life. Even when I made those decisions I regret.

I feel peace knowing that He has a plan and I just need to follow His guidance. And when I stray, He will gently lead me back on course.

I thank Him daily for all the blessings in my life.

* * *

*Take a moment to reflect and write down your thoughts. Note pages are available in the back of the book.*

## CHAPTER 3

## *Patience*

W hen I interviewed for my first management job I was asked, "What is your greatest weakness?"

I didn't hesitate—Patience.

I was then asked if this was "in a good way or a bad way." This caused me to pause. What is the difference?

The clarification: Was I impatient with myself in reaching my goals or was I impatient with other people.

Well, my first thought was BOTH! I had to face the reality that once I made a decision, I expected it to happen yesterday.

As an example, I decided that I wanted a red couch in my family room. I went to three different furniture stores and each one had a red couch.

They would not, however, sell me their floor model; they would have to order one and it would take up to six weeks to be delivered.

At the last store I went to, I expressed my desire to purchase the floor model, and that I had left the other two competitors' stores because the answer was no. This smart salesperson sold me the floor model.

While this may seem like a silly example, it shows my weakness in full color.

On a bigger scale, with both my children and colleagues at my agency, I had some serious work to do.

The first exercise was to stop holding my breath. You know what I mean! That moment when you have heard enough, and you just want the situation to move forward. The moment when you stop listening and start forming your response in your head but have to wait for the person to stop talking.

My first agency was a complete train wreck. I'm still not sure why they gave me the job when my weakness was patience. They must have thought an impatient person would fix things quickly—or some other insane idea.

The manager before me left three months prior to my start date and taken half the team with him. The administrative assistant was out on disability leave. There was a temp worker in her place who had no knowledge of the business so she could hardly do more than take a message. The sales representatives that stayed were either ready to leave without proper leadership or struggled with how to define integrity.

Needless to say, I was holding my breath a lot.

I made hard and fast decisions that definitely hit people the wrong way. Those who were on the fence left within days. The others were terminated for integrity issues. I still had no admin support.

This was truly going to be a lesson in patience. I needed a plan. I needed a timeline. I needed help!

During this time, there was no field training or mentor program for managers. Basically, if you were a great sales rep and you interviewed well, then BOOM you're running an agency.

Apparently, as a new manager you get the worst agency and a "Good luck!" And for me, throw in an extra lesson: working on patience.

I can tell you I never prayed for patience again.

After two months in this nightmare, I was ready to throw

in the towel. I had no sales reps, no admin help, 2,000 clients to serve, and five children starting new schools. Since it was spring when we moved, school had just let out and my children didn't have friends or summer plans. I was working 12-15-hour days. The honeymoon was over.

I was angry at my supervisor, feeling like he had set me up to fail. How in the world could anyone fix this mess? It was a like a wet knot in a shoelace with the sneaker stuck on your foot!

Then, two amazing things happened.

Someone answered my internal job post for the administrative position. She had years of experience working within the company, which meant she knew our systems and our products, and she was willing to move. I hired her immediately. Before she hung up from the only interview we had, I asked her, "What is your name?"

She wouldn't be able to start for another month, but she was undoubtably the first sign of hope.

I struggled along without her for another 30 days and remember the excitement the night before her first day.

I had piled her desk high with immediate service concerns along with many "need to return" phone call slips.

"Finally," I thought, "Help."

And then she cried.

My impatience in full bloom. I didn't take the time to get to know her or ask her how her move was. Did she like the area? Could I help with places to rent or all the little things that come with moving to a new city? NOPE, didn't ask any of those questions. I was all about the workload.

We muddled through that first day together and became a great team fast. I thank God for her every day. I'm thankful she didn't run out screaming on that first day.

She became my patience for the next 15 years.

Her ability to handle my impatience with a simple, "You're

holding your breath" saved me from making many poor decisions.

I am forever in her debt.

The second amazing thing was when I stood up for myself.

This may not sound like a big deal, but it took all my courage.

With no corporate help, I was still trying to figure out how I could turn this beast around. I made a phone call that would change everything.

As one of only two women in my current position companywide, I felt defeated asking for help. Did the new male managers have to ask? Did they really think I could just do this by myself? Would they fire me if I asked for help? Would they think they hired the wrong person for the job?

I thought long and hard about the conversation I was going to have with my supervisor. I practiced my words, even writing down my key points. I would not hold my breath!

I was ready!

I picked up the phone, dialed his number with my hands shaking, half hoping he didn't answer. The minute I heard his voice I said, "I QUIT!"

So much for poise and patience.

Thankfully, he had already fine-tuned *his* patience. He quietly listened as I dumped my bucket all over him.

Was he setting me up to fail? I needed help to get this agency back under control before I could even think about growing a successful team. I am spending my days fielding client service calls trying to retain what clients we had after most of the team had gone left to join the competition! Maybe he should just formally assign all these clients to me and find someone else to fix this mess!

None of these comments were on my notecards. Great! Now he was going to think I'm just a crazy woman!

He remained calm through this entire conversation, never once interrupting me. He actively listened to all my concerns and frustrations. He repeated my issues in confirmation and asked questions when I stopped to take a breath.

This was one of the many things I learned from him: always remain calm. Don't become defensive, instead, actively listen.

When the wind was out of my sails, he told me that he believed I was still the right person for the job. He said I was tough as nails, and he appreciated that I called to ask for help.

The next day he sent two underwriters to work out of my office to relieve some of the pressure from client service issues. He also started spending more time helping me navigate the parts of my job that were most important—rebuilding the team.

My first thought was to question why he didn't set this up to begin with. He knew the mess I was in and that I was new to the position. Why wait until I lost my cool?

Herein lies a basic but very important lesson. Men tend to think differently than women. More often, men are problem-solving thinkers. They don't discuss problems until they have the solution. They don't assume there is a problem unless you tell them. In my experience, women generally need to talk through problems. We don't need someone to fix it, but we do need to speak out loud and discuss the problem.

I have also heard that men can't read our minds. This is probably a good thing since they would be baffled with the multi-tasking that is ever-present for professional women who are also mothers.

In my management career I learned not to "settle" when things got tough. I learned to ask for help and continue to ask questions when you don't understand or need additional information.

The fear of asking is far less than the fear of not knowing!

Everything wasn't all rosy and perfect after that phone call. However, we were headed in a forward direction as a team (finally), and I could see a speck of light at the end of the tunnel.

In working on my weakness, patience, I didn't make those "dump your bucket" calls often after that first call. I would compose an email when I was upset or frustrated and then leave it for a day.

My mother always said that things will feel different in the morning light. I thought this was a ridiculous saying. How could that happen when all the facts are the same? Well, once again she was right.

If I still felt the need to send that email the next day, I would edit out all the bad words and send it. Usually, I deleted the email and gave myself permission to call and ask calm and reasonable questions.

Patience, I found, was about *time*.

I needed to give myself time to really consider an issue without an emotional attachment.

When my children would break the rules, I needed to learn not to discuss or punish in anger or frustration. This was extremely difficult. Teaching them what it took me years to learn, patience in all situations, was not an easy task.

I did learn that it was more effective to tell them I needed time to think about our discussion and/or punishment. The worst thing for them was the wait. Second to that was my statement of how disappointed I was in their decision. At times, that was punishment enough.

Patience is about time, and time needs a strategy.

A well-written strategy can help alleviate that sense of impatience.

I will confess that I only learned to effectively write a true plan and strategy after continual education.

I could have a plan or a goal in my head but keeping up with the daily focus was difficult. I knew there had to be a way to maintain my focus, but I struggled with life stepping in and distracting me.

I knew that in order to work on patience I needed to find a way to set the goal, work on it daily, and find accountability if I ever wanted to move my goal forward.

Fortunately, my company hired some great leaders who saw the need for this as well. They brought in some great trainers throughout my management career that presented numerous ways to strategize your business.

I soaked up the teachings of Troy Korsgarten, Isaac Tolpin, Walter Bond, Ron Wellington, Joe Jordan, and other industry greats.

Years of listening to their formulas to strategize not just their short-term goals, but long-term plans, helped me define my style of planning.

Where did I envision myself in five years? A goal set out this far is easy because it's a long way off.

The next part isn't so easy. What would I need to accomplish this vision on a yearly, monthly, weekly, and daily basis?

This wasn't just for my professional life, I needed it for my personal life as well.

Some of the goals to reach the five-year vision should be left blank. This needs to be a fluid document that I can look at and add to. Life itself is fluid, and when writing such a long-term vision you can't possibly know every piece that will help you achieve the vision.

An example of this happened 12 years ago.

I had written out a goal to retire at age 55, which would give me 30 years with my current company.

I figured out the money side: pension, health insurance and additional savings needed to retire early. Basically, all the math stuff. I had ten years to go, so this was the easy part.

The actual implementation was much harder, and I had to constantly hold myself accountable to the plan. Max out my 401K, increase production to increase income (this had its own strategy), purchase a Long-Term Care policy to protect my retirement income and try to put 10% of my take home into a retail mutual fund account that would be available prior to using my IRA funds.

PHEW!

I left a couple blank spots where my goals to reach the vision were, remembering the lesson of keeping this fluid.

Ten years prior to writing this out, I married my happily ever after. I told him the dollar amount we would need to retire comfortably. He laughed at me and agreed, but he didn't really believe we could do it.

I didn't write out a strategy at that time. Just saying it out loud and knowing we had 20 years to go would give it legs, right?

We went through the first ten years of our marriage blending families and celebrating when we got through Christmas and still had money in our checking. When I finally got around to writing out the retirement vision, ten years had gone by, and we weren't any closer to my "out loud" statement.

Once the vision and the strategies for "10 years to retire-ment" were written out it was time to start some serious implementation. And boy, was that hard!

We didn't have a lot of disposable income at the time, so we had to be creative and start small.

Around the same time, my parents decided to take to the road and live in a motorhome. They loved the deserts of Arizona and wanted to be mobile. "Living our best life" is how my adventurous father put it.

I went to visit them in the place they were currently calling home and was more than a little upset about the location. They were a helicopter ride away from emergency health care. Dad has a bad heart! What were they thinking? I asked them if they would stay in this remote RV park in the *middle of nowhere* if something happened to one of them?

They answered at the same time. A "no" from Dad and a

"yes" from my strong, independent, sometimes stubborn Mom.

Okay, they are the parents. They got this, right? But as their child, I was worried. I called my older brother to discuss the situation. He described a place he had driven through the month before. It was just a couple hours from where our parents were currently. He called it an oasis, and "wouldn't it be great" if we went in on it together to purchase a home there. Mom and Dad could live there, and we all could work on getting the house just right.

That all sounded good but who was going to discuss with the parents? Would they move?

Here is where the "blank" strategy for my retirement strategy was filled in.

"Second home in Arizona."

We found a fixer upper and just like that we had a second home. Getting the parents to agree to move in is another story, but thankfully they did move in. They helped with kickstarting the repairs and put a lot of sweat equity into what would become our family home in Arizona.

God has his own plan for my family and me, and thankfully this piece that he added to my ten-year vision gave us more time with my father.

Six months after we closed on the house Dad had a major heart attack, his third. If they were still living in neverland, he would have died waiting for the helicopter.

*Thank you, God.*

I often hear women talk about time management. There are so many things to accomplish in a day as both professionals and mothers. How can we make it manageable? How can we be there for everyone? Where is the balance between work and family?

Looking back over the past 30 years, I can tell you that I did not perfect time management. I don't know if there is a perfect balance.

Perfect balance to me was a 50/50 split of my time between family and career. To me, it's an impossible feat.

When I realized that balance and time management was something you looked back on to gauge success, my impatience lessened.

There were times when my career demanded 100% of my time. There were times that my family needed 100% of my time.

During these moments of "crisis," the guilt of not balancing is enormous, especially for a working mom.

If the crisis is family, then you feel guilty about work. If the crisis is work, you feel guilty about family.

Such is the life of a working mom.

I was fortunate to work with a company that honored family. It helped to lessen the guilt during family crises but didn't diminish the job that needed to be done.

The key to successful work/life balance is support from people you trust.

Who are those people at work and in your personal life that you can call on during these times of crisis? Those times when you are forced to give 100% to just one place.

Do you have someone who will run to your side when the crisis is family?

Do you have someone who can count on *you* to drop everything and run to their side?

Have you hired people that have a strength that is your weakness?

Have you trained those people to give them the confidence in themselves to act without you present?

For me, asking for help during a crisis is not easy.

Another famous Nita saying, "I'm fine." Even when I really wasn't. It takes courage and patience to step back and realize you're not fine and you need help.

This doesn't make you weak! It makes you stronger!

I love the phrase "My Tribe." We have come so far as

women to realize we need other women in our daily lives to help us.

Who is part of your tribe?

Years ago, an executive with my company approached me about the idea of forming a women support group for women in the field. As a company full of male executives, they were struggling with how to recruit, retain and support women in the field.

I loved this idea!

This was before "My Tribe" theory, and I knew that other women leaders in the field were having the same struggles I was.

Thankfully, we now had ten women managers out of 120. This amazing group of women were eager to get together and share stories of success and failure.

It wasn't easy at first. We hesitated to open up, not really knowing what the company expected of us. Once we decided that we would just support each other no matter what, the group took off.

These women became my tribe. No topic of conversation was off limits. I can't begin to express my gratitude for these ladies. I felt they understood me and had my back. It was letting the breath you were holding in, out. I had been holding that breath for years.

This group still exists today and now includes all women in the field, not just leaders. It has grown into a mentorship and leadership development program.

It took one brave leader to say "we don't know what we don't know" to bring us together and help us grow. He took a chance. He asked for help. I am grateful to him for his help in finding the support I needed to help balance my life.

Reminders:
Patience is time
Time needs a vision

Vision needs a strategy
Be fluid
Hold yourself accountable
Educate yourself
Find support

Is patience still my weakness? YES! However, I can now order furniture and wait the six weeks for delivery.

Progress!

\* \* \*

*Take a moment to reflect and write down your thoughts. Note pages are available in the back of the book.*

# CHAPTER 4

## Inner Strength

I have what?!

It was obvious to me that those who said this about me either didn't really know me, couldn't read my mind, or were just being nice.

I believe my inner strength was born when I learned to actively listen and remain calm in all situations. This only took most of my life to learn.

As a mother of eight and leader of a business, I always felt like I was running around with my hair on fire.

What would I walk into at the office today? What would I come home to? These were constant questions and fears.

There were several times when it was apparent I didn't have the inner strength traits to remain calm.

When my oldest son was 16, I came home from a tough day at the office and started barking orders. Is your homework done? Is your room clean? Why is this living room a mess? Why is your little brother crying? And on and on.

He reached down and threw me over his shoulder, took me to my room and set me on my bed. He looked me in the eye and said, "You really need to calm down."

The nerve! I was going to ground him forever.

Then I realized he was right.

All five of my children still living at home had done the best they could. On top of that, they were all looking forward to me coming home, but I came with work still on my mind, acting like a tornado.

How often had I done this? What example was I setting?

This was the beginning of drawing on my inner strength to remain calm in as many situations as possible.

I won't say I was 100% successful, probably not even 50% in the beginning, but I became aware of the fact that no one else needed to bear the brunt of my stress.

I worked on being present in my current surroundings daily, trying to train my mind not to drift to other tasks or situations while dealing with someone. This can be difficult as a working mom because we have so much to do—and all of it is whirling around in our heads 24/7.

Another of my sons was great at catching me when my mind would drift during our conversations. He would inject ridiculous words into the conversation to test my active listening skills. One of my favorites: "Then a rainbow-colored unicorn danced with the dinosaur." He wouldn't change the tone of his voice, or upset the flow of conversation, just inject silliness to catch me. I must admit I didn't always catch him at it. If I would answer with a "hmmm" or a "that's nice" he wouldn't judge or become upset with me. He would just walk away with a "We'll talk later Mom."

Key lesson: Be where you are when you're there! This was both physical and mental for me. It took lots of practice and every ounce of my inner strength at times.

During a particular time of crisis in our family I had to repeat this to myself over and over, multiple times a day.

I was still new to the manager role, less than a year in this position, when disaster hit our family.

One of my daughters had been sexually abused by a close family member. Our world blew apart.

How could I have allowed this to happen? How could I have put my daughter in a situation that caused this devastation? It felt like I would never be able to put the pieces of our life back together.

Each child had their own questions and fears.

I didn't have a chance to focus solely on my daughter, I had to be present in each of my children's lives so they knew we would move through this together and they weren't alone in their thoughts.

Every conversation with each child was different and heartbreaking. The guilt I felt was overwhelming. My inner strength was tapped, yet still I needed to stand tall and support my children. I still had a job, a big job, to report to every day. The thought of leaving my children even for a moment during this time was almost unbearable.

Our family dinner time was normally a time each day where we shared our days and where laughter was constant. Each child would tell us what the best and worst part of their day was. We connected as a family during this time. Now the table was quiet – everyone afraid to say what was on their minds. *I* was afraid to ask how their day was. We needed help.

In the evenings, I would try to sit with each child individually and discuss their day. I would try to answer their questions honestly to help alleviate their fears.

Questions like, "Is this really true?" "Will we be able to see [this family member] again?" "How can I still feel love for this person after they hurt my sister?" "How can I have both of them in my life now?"

These were tough questions for them to ask and just as tough for me to answer. I had to focus on not just the day but the moment. I could not let my mind go to what this situation would become in a week or month.

I felt like my inner strength was tapped. I felt like I could be running screaming at any given moment.

I didn't have answers to some of these difficult questions.

Their eyes would search my face for clues. I tried so hard not to let them see the fear I was feeling. Most times I would just hold them close and tell them we would get through this together. I had to reassure them constantly that we would always be together.

We needed help.

As I have mentioned, I am huge proponent of family and individual counseling. This, I believe, is what saved us and got us through this unbelievable crisis.

The choice to get counseling for the daughter who was "directly" abused was a no-brainer. She needed more than I could give her to deal with all the thoughts and fears she was going through. I say "directly" not to minimize the terror and pain she was going through, but to relay that abuse by a close family member affects the entire family.

During one of her counseling sessions, her therapist asked me who *I* was seeing for support. I had no answer. Quite frankly, I had enough on my plate and no time to worry about me. How wrong I was.

Of the five children still at home during this crisis, three were in counseling. The other two would tell me, "Don't worry Mom. I'm okay." I was so desperate to have them all be okay that I accepted their answer.

Again, how wrong I was.

I was living in a new city, with no family nearby and no support. When my family would call to check on us, I would tell them we were okay and doing the best we could. I didn't want them to worry.

I realized I was giving them the same answer the two of my children were giving me. I knew I wasn't ok, so how could I just believe they were.

I found a counselor for me the next day.

It would take years for us all to heal from this crisis. For some of us, it became a cancer that tore us apart for a time. For others, saying "I'm ok" turned into additional crises later.

The impact of abuse leaves lasting scars. The scars are different for each of my children. Like most scars, they are hidden and seldom discussed, but when you do see them, the hurt resurfaces.

Through counseling and learning to communicate effectively with each other, we built walls around our inner strength. We moved forward over time. We got through this crisis together.

Sometimes as women we pretend.

For a long time, I pretended to be calm. People believed I had inner strength and could manage any situation. After all, I had a huge career and was raising a large family. You have to be strong to do that, right?

Throughout my career, I never spoke about what was happening in my personal life. I kept these two parts of my life separate, or at least tried hard to. Co-workers would say I only had one emotion or that I was tough as nails. I took this as a compliment—I was good at compartmentalizing my life, or at least looking like I was.

On the outside, I was professional and calm, while on the inside, I felt messy. Not just through a current crisis, but most of the time. Again, trying to be all things to all people *and* work on myself constantly was tiring.

When people ask me how I was successful at my career and managed to raise eight children, I can honestly say I took it one day at time, one crisis at a time, and sometimes one moment at a time. I tried to remain calm as I could, even if that was only on the outside.

I believe inner strength comes from the experience we endure in our lives.

I never gave myself credit for my inner strength. It's easy now to look back and see my inner strength at work.

As I was pretending to be strong, I learned to be strong. That gives a whole new meaning to "fake it 'til you make it."

I love when God puts people in your life who say something that instantly changes your perspective. Sometimes those people are in your life for a very short time, maybe just so you can hear those words.

Towards the end of my management career, I was interviewing a candidate to join my team. My interview skills were more conversational than question-oriented after so many years.

As we were discussing her fear of taking on a new and completely different career path than she had ever experienced, she made a comment that changed my perception on inner strength and fear.

"Your body reacts the same to both fear and excitement. Your hands shake, your heart races and your tummy flips around."

She was right!

While others saw me as strong, I had some big fears that started holding me back. I couldn't tell people I was afraid because I feared they would think I was weak. I had started avoiding situations in my professional life that would cause a fear reaction.

After hearing that interviewee's words, every time I would start to be fearful, I would tell myself I was excited—even if I knew I was only *pretending* to be excited.

As with most people, public speaking was my biggest fear.

On the outside, I appeared "tough as nails;" on the inside, doubt would take up residency and thoughts of "if they really knew me" swirled in my head.

Anytime I had to do any public speaking, I was a mess. People were going to see that I really didn't have my shit together. Their view of me as a strong, professional woman would be shattered.

It often felt like I was on a rollercoaster that I couldn't get off. I hate rollercoasters. I was racing forward with no escape, getting ready to race straight down and, in my mind, probably crash and die.

My fear held me back.

Then, as a dear friend used to say, "God winked."

Someone who truly believed in me asked me to step into a role that would require me to speak in front of large groups of people on a regular basis.

This was a role that at one time in my career I aspired to achieve. I had approached my leadership about this goal before but was told that he couldn't see me doing anything other than my current role. This was a person I trusted, so if he couldn't see me performing well, then what made me think I *could*? I let the goal go. It was honestly a relief knowing the expectations for public speaking while I still harbored that fear —so "PHEW," was my thought at the time.

What we fear is what holds us back. Every time! I heard this from a keynote speaker at a company conference not to long before my "God winked" moment. No truer words have ever been spoken.

I had served 22 years as a manager and was just months away from my retirement goal date when my supervisor called me about taking on the role I'd once aspired to be in. I knew I had to be honest with him about my fears.

He is one of the kindest, most honest men I have ever met. He is the type of leader you would walk through fire for.

When he laid out his plan to move our company forward, I knew there was no way I could allow my fear to stand in his way.

Off on that rollercoaster I went!

I shifted my attitude to excitement rather than fear when it came to public speaking. I began starting each "talk" by telling the group I was shaking with excitement to talk to them. I drew on my inner strength every time. I won't say I perfected the skill of public speaking, but I did overcome the paralyzing fear.

It took total belief in someone else's vision to get me to this place. I knew I had to do my part. Like most woman, if you are doing it for someone else, it's easier to say "yes" regardless of your fears.

At my last event, I was speaking to a large group of women in Atlanta. I was the emcee for a day long retreat where the focus was empowering women. It was a wonderful day with an amazing group of women. I prayed my message would mean something to them and hoped even just one lesson might help them in their professional goals. If I could help someone, I would feel the day was a success.

When the meeting ended, a beautiful soul came up to me and said, "Someday I want to be as strong and confident as you are."

Wow! I still felt the same fears inside, but by turning my fear into excitement, I had reached this woman. It was a defining moment for me.

I replied to her, "You already are, you just have to believe."

Think about a time in your life when you had to be strong. How did you tap into your inner strength? Do people see you as a calm leader?

My husband has a fear of flying, and I remember on one particularly rough flight, he was a mess. Right down to his sweaty hands and heart palpitations. It was a long, bumpy ride from beginning to end. After a couple hours of him firmly gripping my hand and telling me he loved me like he wasn't going to make it, I looked at him and said, "Look at the flight attendants. They are calm. It's going to be ok."

Do people see you as the calm flight attendant? Do your children?

Believe in yourself and your inner strength. It's in there! I promise!

* * *

*Take a moment to reflect and write down your thoughts. Note pages are available in the back of the book.*

CHAPTER 5

*Humor*

Humor is an interesting word.

It can be used as medicine, through laughter.

It can be used at your expense.

It can be used in judgement of others.

It can be used as a defense mechanism.

In other words, it can bring out the best and worst in us.

I grew up in a funny and witty family. Laughter was a daily sound in our home. We would laugh at ourselves and each other. There is no better feeling than a good, old-fashioned belly laugh!

We learned not to take ourselves so seriously, and when we were the brunt of the joke, to laugh along. Not always an easy thing to do as a kid—or as an adult. Even yet, it's better than getting mad and throwing a fit.

Kids can be mean. Especially when you are the little girl of French descent with a unibrow and a mustache better than most boys twice your age.

I remember coming home from school one day in tears because some boy teased me about my mustache. My Dad promptly reassured me I was beautiful, and those boys probably like me but didn't know how to tell me. I was around ten years old, so boys were just mean and stupid in my eyes.

He then took me into the bathroom and shaved my mustache off! Boy was he in trouble when Mom got home. She yelled at him that now it would grow back *thicker!* What?! The tears came flowing again. Were they going to allow their ten-year-old to shave every day? It is a very vivid memory for me.

The mustache did come back and thicker than ever, I'm convinced. But my father's words stuck with me more than anything, *I was beautiful*. Even if I didn't see it, he did. I wore that mustache proudly until I was about 30 and discovered waxing.

Laughter at another's expense is rarely a good thing. They may laugh along with you but trust me they are not laughing on the inside.

Growing up with one eyebrow, a mustache, and a last name that was mainly associated with an athletic support device (Jock) undeniably gave me thick skin.

I would need this thick skin working in a male-dominated industry.

If you didn't laugh along with the lewd jokes and sexual innuendos, you were considered a prude and excluded from after-hours discussions. As a new manager, I learned after hours is when the real solutions to our daily lives were discussed and resolved. Not that we didn't learn during the workday meetings, but the unofficial meetings had more guts, more honesty, and the fear of asking questions in a group were gone.

As a former bartender, walking into a hotel bar full of men who were my peers never intimidated me. However, finding a way into a conversation that may turn into unwanted comments about my appearance or my bedroom skills was both irritating and intimidating.

These were men I admired for their ability to do our job

and do it well. I wanted to hear what they had to say about the general meetings and how they were going to implement the new strategies we just learned.

At the time, it seemed the only way to do this was to laugh along with their misogynistic jokes and make witty comments in retaliation when they went too far.

On the inside, I wished they would see me as a peer, not a woman. It felt like I was allowing them to treat me as a second-class citizen rather than standing up for myself. I couldn't take the chance that they wouldn't allow me to be part of their real conversation. So, I put up with demeaning comments like:

"You must be good in bed."

"Can you scratch my back?"

"You're single, he's single. You guys should get together."

"No one has to know if we sleep together."

I used laughter as a defense mechanism in most situations. In reality, they made me sick to my stomach. I felt like an object for their amusement.

I became smarter over the years and could gauge when it was time to leave these valuable after-hours discussions. When the laughter was getting louder, it was time to leave.

Not all the men I worked with made these sexist comments. I also started to realize I was only encouraging them by joining in on their laughter. I realize now I should have stood up for myself more often instead of laughing along.

One time stands out above the rest. While it started with an unbelievable request, it turned into one of my biggest blessings.

I had been in my new role for less than a year, and a company dinner was coming up. My supervisor, who was recently divorced, planned to bring his new girlfriend, and he requested that I bring a date to the dinner so his new girl-friend wouldn't "think there was anything going on between us."

What?! Initially, I thought he was joking, so I changed the

subject, only to have him ask me again to bring a date later in the conversation.

Let me get this straight: I'm a single mom with five kids at home and an intense job I'm still wrangling with, and you want me to find a date? What was I supposed to do, stand on the corner with a sign? Ask my employees if they had a friend? *Good grief!*

As the dinner approached, my supervisor again reached out to make sure I brought a date. I said, "A friend," to end the conversation. Later that day, I called a male friend I had known for quite a few years who lived in a different state. He was a 6'4 redheaded welder who would no doubt not fit into the group I was going to ask him to escort me to. But he knew me well and would understand this crazy situation.

His answering machine picked up and not knowing how to explain the situation I just said, "I need a man!"

He was a true friend and didn't ask a lot of questions. He said he would borrow a jacket and tie and fly up the night before the event. I was embarrassed, but grateful.

He did fly in the day before, but we didn't attend the event. Instead, we stayed up all night talking, and our relationship started to change.

After ten years of close friendship, he became my Happily Ever After and now, we've been married 20 years.

As the years went by, a new group of men joined the leadership team. These men stood up to lewd comments and became like brothers to me.

I confided in one of the new leaders about one of these lewd comments. When he said he would speak to a supervisor, I was surprised I was more scared by that than the inappropriate comments themselves. I had grown numb to it by now. I didn't want to be considered a prude or a tattletale, and I was terrified of the "she's lying" debate. Not to mention the years I spent avoiding exclusion from those conversations I knew would ultimately help my team grow and succeed.

I made him promise he wouldn't say anything, and he agreed. After that, I noticed he would make a point to join conversations I was in. At one point even stepping between a peer and me when the peer was getting too close.

Later, I learned he did say something to the comment-maker's supervisor. He made sure it was known he would not tolerate "middle school" attitudes; he knew that if he didn't step up no one would. None of my fears came true—no one avoided me.

I wish I could say that *I* finally said "enough." However, it was this group of men, my brothers, who I credit with that. They stood up to those commenters. They said "Enough".

The changes they made, and continue to make, in our beloved company are noticeable. I wasn't the only woman who felt this way and I truly believe it was holding women back in our company for too long. Not anymore.

These men, my brothers, are truly amazing humans. I am forever grateful for their respect and friendship.

Humor is an interesting word.

I choose to laugh at myself. I choose to laugh at those funny memories and remember fondly the moments when a good belly laugh solved the day's troubles.

I may have learned to have thick skin, but more importantly, I learned to be kind.

* * *

*Take a moment to reflect and write down your thoughts. Note pages are available in the back of the book.*

## CHAPTER 6

*Perceptions of Perfection*

U p to this point, we've walked through several stories of mistakes I've made, and discovered the lessons we learn through these mistakes make us who we are. That all mistakes or falls help us develop traits that can become our lifelines for the rest of our lives.

The bottom line is we all make mistakes: we misjudge situations and we definitely overreact. I've come to realize there are two simple phrases that will correct these misjudgments or mistakes:

"I'm sorry"

"I was wrong"

These statements are far easier to write than to say. I realized I didn't use these statements enough as a mom when one of my sons, at the age of ten, brought it to my attention. We were having a heated discussion about a frivolous chore I had asked him to do: sort the sock box.

In a home with so many children, laundry was a constant chore. One that usually kept me up late at night and seemed impossible to catch up on. All moms know the fury of clean clothes tried on once and only to end up in the dirty clothes pile unworn. UGH!

Socks were the one thing I refused to fold or sort. It became the "punishment" for an infraction—the dreaded sock box!

On this occasion, my son told me all the socks were matched and he was done. But still seeing a sizeable pile of unmatched socks, I told him to look again. I know the dryer eats socks, but it was impossible to have *that* many without a match. He continued to argue that he had put the socks away and the pile was what was left.

Exasperated, I thought he was pulling a fast one. I sat down and started going through the pile with him to prove him wrong. If I found one more match, he was in big trouble.

However, he was right: none of the remaining socks matched. Suddenly, the pile didn't look as large as when I started this discussion. I looked in the sock drawer in my room and there was a neat row of matched socks.

I looked at his scowling you-never-believe-me face, and said, "You were right. I was wrong. I'm sorry."

The look on his face immediately changed to shock. "What did you say?!"

I repeated, "I was wrong. I'm sorry."

My ten-year-old baby jumped and yelled for the whole house to hear, "Mom said she was wrong!! Mark the calendar!" as he danced around the living room.

My first reaction was to be a little angry, but soon I realized he was right. I rarely—if ever—told my children I was wrong or I was sorry. By always taking the stance that I was the parent, and therefore always right, I wasn't teaching my children how to correct their own mistakes.

From the mouth of babes.

This, like most lessons I learned as a mother, flowed over to my work life.

How many times did I assume that I, as the boss, know more than my employees?

What perception was I giving that I was always right or "perfect" to my children or my team?

I tried harder after that day to be a better listener (a daily exercise). I also worked on admitting I was wrong rather than justifying my stance. Of course, getting good at this doesn't happen overnight. -being self-aware is half the battle!

I wonder if my son realizes the powerful life skill he taught me that day. I'm not sure I have ever told him. Maybe now is the time.

One of my faults, or maybe I should say "perfectionist traits" is that I am a big dreamer. Big dreamers are people who can look to the future and not only see their perception of perfection, but they can feel it.

Most times big dreamers skip some important steps to that big dream with an abundance of over confidence.

Over confidence?

Looking back on some of my big dreams, I can see where I not only jumped, but gaily skipped over, crucial steps and ignored red flags in pursuit of that big dream.

My life in 1994 was perfect...in my perception.

My insurance business was rocking. I was the top sales rep for the entire company the year before—one of the first women to accomplish this lofty goal.

I was married to #2, who was also running his own business very successfully. He had been sober for several years. We still had our ups and downs—as most couples and families do —but my perception of our lives is that we were doing great.

I was making more money than I could ever have imagined and became very involved in our small community.

I met with my accountant in the Fall of 1994 for pre-tax planning, and in this conversation, my big-dreamer self went into overdrive.

"If you don't spend $35,000 on one of the businesses by year's end, you will end up paying the IRS $45,000."

Never tell a big dreamer to spend that kind of money! Immediately, I developed a great idea!

#2's business included flooring installation. He could install, mend, or design *anything* when it came to flooring. His work was in demand for both residential and commercial properties.

I have always loved interior design, but it did not become my occupation.

What if we combined our two talents and opened a home interior store? The perfect store front with huge alcove windows just became vacant in our beautiful downtown.

I could see it perfectly in my mind: I would change out the front window displays with new wallpaper, flooring, and furniture on loan from a local furniture store. People would see the beautiful displays and want them in their home. The mayor's wife was an artist, I could commission her to do a matching art piece and raffle off for charity.

There were other flooring, paint, and home décor stores in town but none of them had it "all" in one place.

We would have a private opening for the town dignitaries by invitation only!

With a large Hispanic population, we would focus on hiring bilingual employees to ensure we could reach an untapped market.

The second story would be a window-covering heaven with faux windows along the wall in all different shapes, sizes, and colors!

We would run different types of commercial carpet halfway up the high walls downstairs with complementary colors of paint above them.

People wouldn't just see beautiful creations in magazines and brochures, they would see it in real life!

Excitedly, I laid out the plan to the hubby. I could work both locations as we get the new business off the ground. My insurance business is what paid the bills, and I had an amazing staff that would cover me.

He responded to my well-laid-out BIG DREAM with, "No way. There is no way we can start a third business."

A seasoned salesperson, I talked him into it. We spent the next six months putting together my Big Dream. It was everything I imagined. It was also the beginning of the end.

The end of his sobriety, the end of our financial stability, and the end of our marriage.

The first six months of designing, planning, and hiring were exciting. I thought there was nothing we couldn't accomplish.

Our private opening was a huge success. The store was just as beautiful as I imagined. The front alcove windows were the showcase I had dreamt of. Everything was perfect.

Except the fact that my big dreamer self didn't really listen to the concerns and fears my husband had in the beginning.

Sobriety is a fragile thing. Stress or change can smash it to pieces and once broken, it can go downhill *fast*.

I went back to my insurance business after the first six months but continued working at the store in the evenings and on weekends. I loved being there. I loved changing the showroom and talking to customers about their dreams of interior decorating.

What I didn't do, was keep in touch with business finances. Whenever I would inquire, the answer was usually, "We are about to land a new commercial account and then we will be set."

I was so naïve and trusting that I didn't see what was happening right in front of me.

Within 18 months, not only was my big dream shattered into a million pieces, but so was my life.

My husband was no longer sober. He was having an affair with the manager of a new commercial account and our overdue taxes and debt obliterated any savings and assets we had.

Was all this inevitable without the store? I will never know that answer. If I had listened to his fears and concerns, maybe things would have turned out differently.

What I saw as perfection in that big dream was only my perception. What I wanted to see, not the whole picture.

This mistake cost me everything we had built for our family. It would take years to recover from both the emotional and financial toll this mistake—this perception of perfection —caused in our lives.

I won't say I stopped being a big dreamer. I still dream big, but I learned to invest the right amount of time, research, and planning into my big dreams to protect them (and myself).

I learned to write out my vision and work my way backwards to each step needed to make dreams not only become a reality, but a success.

The who, what, when, and where of a good business plan are imperative. Listen to your advisors and even your naysayers. Are their concerns real? Do you have a plan to overcome their concerns? Focusing on your vision can be fruitful with the right plan. I learned not to skip the steps between the vision and the implementation.

Where I *do* see perfection is in my children. Are they totally perfect? No. I see them thriving and parenting so much better than I did. Through all the turmoil life has thrown at them, they stand up to the challenge and meet it head on. They are good people with strong hearts.

That perception of perfect makes all the challenges I faced worth it. I still struggle to forgive myself for those mistakes, but seeing their perfection gets me a little bit closer.

Life is a bumpy ride. No one does it perfectly. You don't need courage for the whole journey right now...just the next step!

Hike up those bra straps, learn from your mistakes, write

out a solid and detailed plan, and be flexible. When you are wrong, stand tall and say, "I'm sorry, I was wrong." You will empower others to also learn from their mistakes.

"Smooth seas do not make a skilled sailor!"
    -Franklin D Roosevelt

\* \* \*

*Take a moment to reflect and write down your thoughts. Note pages are available in the back of the book.*

# CHAPTER 7

# *Motherhood (vs. Childbirth)*

The difference between childbirth and motherhood is astronomic. Childbirth is relatively short, while motherhood is forever.

I have had a hand in raising eight children. I am their mother. For some, I am not the person who gave birth to them, but I am the person who cheered them on, hugged them when they hurt, made sure they had a healthy childhood, and held them accountable to their actions.

Among my eight children there are eight biological parents, not including myself.

To answer the question, "how many children do you have?" has been a source of anxiety for me. Do I say eight or do I just say three because I gave birth to three? Does that mean I don't love the other five as much? People ask the most personal questions when you say you have eight children.

"Are they all yours?"

What in the world does that mean? They aren't my possessions. I didn't borrow them. I was always trying to defer these ridiculous questions and comments with a simple, "yes." That answer, of course, encouraged more curiosity: "Did you actually give birth to eight children?"

Yikes, now we are going to discuss my medical history! What's next, asking if they all have the same father?

I attempted to end these conversations politely and with statements that would convey that I love all eight of my children, period.

And yet, questions that always felt judgmental would continue. What does it matter when or how God put these children in my life? I was entrusted to do the best I could as their mother regardless of who gave birth to them.

"Walk me through all your children and explain where they came from."

What?! These questions didn't come from strangers; they came from people who were in my daily life.

Why do people have a fascination with my motherhood? Do they desire to discredit me?

How about asking me if I financially supported all eight? Did I oversee their health, education, and mental wellbeing? Did I drop everything if they needed me because they were my most important responsibility?

There are so many blended families in the world today, it's time for us to respect each other's family units without seeking explanation.

Okay, jumping off that soapbox but boy, did that feel good!

I worked hard to treat all eight of my children equally and show them each support and love as they were growing up. That was the easiest part.

The hardest part was helping them keep healthy relationships with their bio families.

I truly believe that the more people who love my children, the better off my children would be.

This belief was passed down from my grandfather. It wasn't until my teenage years, at a family reunion, when I learned we weren't biologically related. Someone commented that my grandfather never treated me differently despite.

My response was, "why would he?"

He was the best grandfather. He always listened to my stories, and he was the best hugger. My favorite place as a child was on his lap, listening to his deep laugh. I always felt how much he loved me...always.

I had all the facts to know that he was my step-grandfather. Not everyone had three sets of grandparents in those days. His last name wasn't my father's last name or my mother's maiden name.

None of that mattered. I felt how much my grandfather loved me every day of his life.

I hope that all eight of my children can say they felt that from me.

Childbirth is a lifechanging experience. To create a new life within your body is truly a wonder. Feeling that life move inside of you is a joy. The love, like no other love when you push that baby into the world and the warmth when they first lay that little human on the outside of your body is by far the most amazing feeling I have ever felt.

Raising a child is also a life-changing experience. Watching them grow, thrive, and discover themselves and the world around them is an experience. All the firsts they have felt like my firsts. I wish all women could have that.

Raising children while being the primary breadwinner was challenging. Food on the table and a roof over their heads was sometimes my only focus.

During these lean periods, the fears I faced felt ominous. Along with my fear of whether I could provide for my children came guilt.

I was constantly second-guessing and impatient with my children, and I struggled because I was stressed by my fear of letting them down.

Every mother I have spoken with shares a story of guilt or fear they aren't enough.

My saving grace during these moments of guilt is a very

important question: Am I doing the absolute best I could do? Was there something else I could be doing?

When I realized I was doing the best I could in those moments, I allowed my fears to shrink. I allowed myself to let go of feeling "I'm not enough."

I worked hard to not allow the fears of tomorrow diminish the joys of today. When I was able to do that, it reminded me of being that eight-year-old girl who put glasses on for the first time. I could see things clearer, and my best became better.

Recently, I shared one of my "guilt" stories with one of my sons. I have one of these guilt stories for each of my children. You know, the story where you cringe with guilt when you remember.

He is a father now and mentioned to me how he sometimes feels guilty at times for not "being enough" as a parent or feeling inadequate. He is an incredible father to his three boys, but I remember feeling inadequate, so I told him a story about a time I felt I wasn't enough for him.

We moved to our new city when he was seven years old. At that time, I had five of my children still living at home. He was the youngest and the only child in elementary school.

I was blessed to find a home within walking distance of an elementary, middle, and high school. With my new job, there was no way I would have been able to drop off and pick up every day.

His older sisters were in high school, so they could leave school and meet him when he was released from class and walk him the two blocks to home.

Our schedules were hectic to say the least. New city, new schools, new position within my company, and no family around. We had no time to meet neighbors.

On one of these hectic days, we had a total communication breakdown. My seven-year-old wasn't met by his sisters. He decided to walk the two blocks in the pouring rain but had no way to get into the house because I never thought to give him a key. He also didn't know my new work number and of course we didn't have cell phones then.

A kind neighbor came out to see if he wanted to come inside her house and wait for his sisters, but I had taught him to not go off with strangers, so he said no.

My baby stood in the pouring Oregon rain for an hour before his sisters came home!

I told him the guilt from that story still makes my stomach turn.

He looked at me after I finished the story and said, "Geez, Mom, I don't even remember that!"

The lesson I learned that day was to release some of the guilt I had been harboring. I did the best I could in most situations. I no longer needed to be perfect.

Guilt is a negative and draining emotion that serves no purpose for me. One of my favorite lessons from years of attending Al-Anon meetings was "Let go!"

There are so many lessons to learn from blended families —the subject could fill two books, at least.

It is not easy. I always tried to treat all my children equally in praise and punishment. The yells of "you're not my mother" have been heard at least a million times in my house.

My "chosen" children (chosen meaning I didn't give birth to them) don't all call me Mom. I was always okay with that. They already had someone they called Mom.

I once had a friend tell me that the thought of his kids calling someone else Dad made his skin crawl.

I explained that parental titles are a *reference* to most children, not a *feeling*.

I learned this one day when, out of curiosity, I asked one of my chosen children why she never called me Mom. She was 5 when God brought her into my life, but now, she was adult.

Her response said it all, "Nita does mean Mom."

I'm so glad I never forced the issue of titles.

I always tried to respect my children's relationship with

their bio parents. At times, I even had the bio parents stay in my home to show a unified front. I never wanted my children to feel they had to choose.

Two months after marrying my Happily Ever After (Hubby #3), the mother of his two children had a time where she could not take care of the children.

It was not a question whether his children would live with us full time. Of my six, only three were still living at home, and one was already a senior in high school. My cousin was also living with us. We were blessed to live in a home large enough for all of us, but the addition of two more people would be a challenge.

When we received the call from the children's grandmother to pick them up, we did not hesitate. While we anticipated a challenge with this arrangement, we jumped in with air mattresses, bunk beds, and makeshift dressers before they arrived.

Obviously, these two kiddos were a mess to say the least. At ages seven and ten, they didn't understand what happened to their mother. Their Dad had just gotten married and moved to another state. They had new siblings they didn't really know, and they were scared.

Their world was completely turned upside down.

I was proud of my kids, watching them jump right in to make their new siblings comfortable. Of course, the honeymoon period didn't last, but I believed they were getting comfortable, even if they were bickering and becoming siblings.

There were a lot of tearful nights. The way I cooked wasn't how their mother cooked. (We still laugh at how all they wanted was Hamburger Helper from a box.) The way I made their lunches wasn't right. Pretty much everything I did was wrong. I realized that they just missed their mom and couldn't understand where she was and why they couldn't talk to her.

The original "just a couple weeks" turned into a month, and we made the decision to pursue full-time custody. This was not an easy discussion for anyone, but these kids needed to start school and they needed stability.

They also needed to know their mom was okay. They needed to see her.

Thanksgiving was right around the corner, and I felt it was the perfect occasion to invite their mom to Oregon. I also wanted her to stay at our house with her children.

I wanted the kiddos to see a unified front, and know they were the most important thing to all three of their parents. Further, I just wanted them to see their mom was going to be okay.

Convincing the hubby that this was a good idea was a long conversation; it took a few days. I can still see the look of shock on his face and hear him saying, "You want my ex-wife to stay at our house?!"

My response was ultimately what convinced him, "No, I want the kids' mother to stay at our house."

Their mom accepted our invitation. The kids were excited to finally be able to see her.

I won't say things went completely smooth. As a matter of fact, our brand-new washer broke down the day before Thanksgiving with a mountain of laundry to do. I spent the day trying to hide the laundry mountain, contemplating whether to go to a laundromat.

The look on those babies' faces made all the uncomfortable moments worth it.

I didn't become friends with my children's mothers, but I respected their relationship with our children. We didn't always agree on rules or lessons that our children needed to learn, but I have no doubt my children's bio moms knew I loved their children, and my door was open for discussion, even if sometimes it was a heated discussion. I always advocated in the best interest of our children.

They didn't all call me Mom, but wherever I was, that was their home.

My grandmother always said when you have a child, it is like having your heart out walking around. That resonates deeply with me. The sense of pride, the need to protect, and the pain of their mistakes are always with you. You don't have to give birth to the child to feel these things.

As I have mentioned, I don't have a daily relationship with all my children. Some have taken a path they know I don't agree with. Choosing to follow the "other" path that leads to addiction. It can be hard to let go of someone you love who makes these choices. However, even after years of not hearing from one my kids, it makes my heart happy to hear from them.

Years ago, my oldest daughter reached out after many years without contact. I was thrilled to hear from her and to know she was safe, but I was also hesitant. The last time we spoke she was asking for money. It was always a difficult conversation where my answer was usually no. Each child was given one "test" loan to prove their credit with me. If the loan was paid back, then their credit was good. If not, then the Bank of Mom was closed.

Instead, what I heard on that call was a mature woman; a mother of three who found her relationship with her Higher Power.

She thanked me for teaching her meaningful lessons about motherhood. Even in her rough years, she always knew there was another path. She was now gratefully on that path.

No matter how long it takes them to choose to make better decisions I feel that by showing my children another way they know they have a choice. I am always happy to hear when it works. I hope to hear this from all of them while I am still on this earth.

Probably the hardest part of a blended family were outbursts of "I want to live with (the other parent)!" These fits usually happened when they were in trouble or didn't like a rule that was imposed on them.

I can't count the number of times the father of two of my children sued me for custody because one of them would call and say how awful life was with me. That is a pain that cut *deep.*

At the time, I was unable to step back and separate the rant and ravings of a pre-teen from my parenting skills.

There were times I thought, "Fine! Go live with the other parent! It would be easier to be the weekend fun parent rather than the one with all the rules."

That response would last a short time and I would realize that it was my job to raise my children. It was the most important job I had. I would fight for them to be in an environment that I created, and that I knew was best for them.

However, most of my children did stay with their other or bio parent for a time. Whether it was visitation, or we decided it was time for them to see "the grass wasn't always greener on the other side," these were hard times for me.

One of my children moved in with her bio father after many years of battling with me. It didn't take long for her to see it wasn't all rosy and she begged me to come home after just a few weeks. As hard as it was, I made her stay until the end of the school semester, talking to her every night and making the drive to see her. It was the best thing I could have done. She never asked again.

Looking back, I am glad I fought so hard to keep my children with me. It would have been easier and less expensive to let them go, but I see the morals and values that I instilled. But damn, was it hard!

While I raised my children, I had special people placed in my life. Some of these people were just in it for a blink, but others were my lifelines. I am grateful for them all.

I am beyond blessed to have had parents I could turn to in the storms that come with motherhood.

I also had two close and dependable friends who would drop everything to come to my aid in a crisis. They were my lifeline through two bad marriages and raising eight children. They were also the people who smiled the biggest when I married my Happily Ever After and added two more beautiful children to my family.

I simply can't imagine how I would have walked through the hardships and trials of my life without them to lean on. I am forever grateful for their love and support. I miss them both very much. When one of them died, the relationship changed.

In trying to help I became too judgmental in decisions that the surviving partner was making. It came off as controlling to her. I needed to step back. We have attempted to talk again which is difficult. I try to end every call with I love you and thank you for all your support in my life.

The man I married began as a friend God put in my life. As friends, we shared the ups and downs of our lives with no intention to become more than friends. There were times during our friendship when he would call, and with just a simple, "How are you?" I'd find myself in tears on the other end. He never asked questions, he just listened to me cry with an occasional "Ssshhhh, it will be ok."

When we decided to marry, I asked him not to be something else I had to get over.

He is my safe place. He is my rock. He is my Happily Ever After.

They say it takes a village to raise children. There were times when I needed the whole village in the boat with me. All hands on deck!

I am most grateful to God for giving me the strength to be the rudder that kept our lives on the best path possible. When I would steer off that path, God would put these people in my life to steer us back—sometimes not so gently.

My children were my constant. Always the reason to push

forward. They taught me so many lessons. Through the eyes of a child, you truly do see life differently. Their happiness, their fears, and their love are pure and real.

I wish I had taken more time to see this when they were younger. Instead, my fears blinded me at times. The fears of my capability to support them, to give us a better life, was all I saw. I wish I had been more patient. I wish I would have actively listened more often.

I believe this defines motherhood: reflecting and wishing I could have been better.

My children rarely saw me cry because I didn't want my fears to be their fears. I was the mom, and I always had to be strong for them. Or at least strong in their eyes.

There were moments when I just couldn't be strong. One of these moments was when my 14-year-old son was arrested... for the first time.

Police officers came to my door at midnight looking for him. I went to his room and saw he was in bed under the covers. I let the officers know he was sleeping so they must have the wrong person. They asked to speak to him.

I went back into his room to wake him. I flipped on the light and called his name two or three times with no answer. Finally, I pulled back the covers to discover the best clothing dummy I had ever seen. Even the arms were positioned over its head the way he usually slept.

The officers asked me to call them immediately when he returned home. I paced for two hours waiting for him when he finally came through the front door.

The officers came back and questioned him. They advised me they had enough information to arrest him, but since he was a minor, I would have to follow them and just bring him home after they booked him.

They clearly wanted to save me from further distress. They could see I was a single mom. The other two teenagers were sitting at the kitchen table, unable to sleep, and obviously no fatherly figure around. The officers' hearts were in the right place.

I made a decision no mother should have to make.

"Arrest him." I said, so quietly to the officer that I had to repeat myself.

They turned to my son, read him his rights, and hand-cuffed him while he looked at me pleadingly.

I stood there holding my breath, knowing if I let it out, I might scream. I didn't want the other kids any more afraid than they already were. I did want them to see the conse-quences of their brother's actions.

After they left with my son in handcuffs, I could no longer hold back. I dropped to the floor and screamed, crying uncon-trollably. How had it come to this?!

This scared my two teenage daughters worse than witnessing their younger brother get arrested. Their shouts of "Mom!! What can we do?! Are you okay?!" brought me around quickly.

This situation made me realize my children needed to see that I was human. How would they learn to handle crisis as adults or parents if they only saw me one way?

I can't say that I showed them drastic examples like that very often, but I did start having conversations about things that upset me and how I would work through them. My chil-dren are adults now and still joke about Mom having one emotion. I'm not sure what one emotion they think I have but my hope is it's a good one.

I wish I had been better.

This son would continue to make poor decisions for the next three years. He was usually the "lookout" so didn't really face hard consequences. He started drinking and using drugs to the extent that I was at the school on a weekly basis because of some stupid thing he did on campus.

I showed up one day to see him sitting with two police officers behind him. One of the officers commented on how polite and cooperative he was. This took me aback, "So I'm raising a polite criminal?!"

His drinking and using came to a head the winter of his senior year of high school. Which, by the way, was a private military school since he was expelled from the public high school the rest of the kids attended.

I received the call no mother wants to receive.

"We have arrested your son for grand theft auto, kidnapping and assault." (And that's just a few of these charges.) He was drunk, and they had him in solitary confinement at juvenile hall.

I could go to see him, but it would be through plexiglass, as he was now considered dangerous.

My heart was broken. I was determined to get him on the right path, and I refused to give up on him.

I found a residential rehab center about 40 miles from where we were living. They wouldn't have an opening for a couple weeks. I made the decision to leave him in solitary confinement at juvenile hall because I knew he obviously wouldn't listen to me or stay home. This had gone beyond any punishment I could give him.

On the day he was to appear before a judge in juvenile court who would determine his consequences, I knew I had to ask for one more chance.

I stood up in front of the judge and assured her that I had found a rehab center for my son. I begged her to give me one more chance to save him. Thankfully, she agreed.

This son has now been sober for almost 20 years. He is a wonderful husband, father, business owner, and son. He credits his life to many things, but always takes the opportunity to thank me for those challenging decisions I had to make.

The luxury of having adult children is the blessing of grandchildren. All the lessons and feelings of "I wish I had been better" give me a second chance. I now understand when adult children ask their parents, "Who are you and what did you do with the person who raised me?"

I can be patient. I can slow down and watch as they discover life. Being a grandmother is truly the favorite season of my life.

When I was getting ready to retire, everyone asked me what I was going to do in retirement. I was always so busy; I don't think they could picture *me* slowing down. My answer was always, "I'm not going to be a box grandma any longer. I'm going to spend as much time as I can making memories with the grandbabies."

A "box grandma" makes an appearance in her grandchildren's lives by sending boxes for special occasions. Of course, I won't stop sending gift boxes. I love putting the boxes together and I know they love getting them. I also know that they love our one-on-one time almost as much as I do.

They make me better.

When the pandemic hit in 2020, I was in a leadership role with my company. Women were more deeply impacted as they navigated how to manage this nightmare within their daily lives.

What started as a temporary pivot, became a permanent change to their work and family life for an indefinite time all too quickly. While for most women, especially professional women who are also mothers, multitasking is second nature, this was entirely different. These women were struggling to maintain their businesses while figuring out how to manage daycare and homeschooling.

I couldn't even imagine!

As I counseled women on my team, I realized they were all feeling the same sense of inadequacy. Most of them were at their breaking point. I wondered if they were just venting to me or if they were talking amongst themselves as well.

The women's support group within our company was the answer to, "I'm not enough."

We started hosting social hours and support meetings for women on our sales team. Choosing women to speak to this group was an easy task for me. I would go to our top-producing women others looked up to. They could share how they were managing the current nightmare they were all in.

When I heard back from my outreach, their reply was all the same: they were struggling. They wondered how they could offer support and guidance when they were trying to get through each day without losing their minds.

One beautiful soul's reply was, "Seriously, Nita! I'm a shit show right now!"

But wasn't everyone? Maybe that's what all these women needed to hear. When I spoke with the amazing women on my team, they would express that they just didn't feel they could do it. It was just too much.

My response to them, and the theme behind our first social hour, was the message they needed:

YOU ARE DOING IT!

Every step forward, in both your business and your family life, was a step. That step was doing it—facing the unbelievable daily challenges of both motherhood and business owner.

This social hour helped them realize they were not alone in their fear of inadequacy.

They were enough!

The response to the social hour was tremendous—for both the participants and the speakers. It was hard to keep up with all the ideas and strategies the women on the call were sharing.

There were tears, laughter, and lots of virtual love. I was so proud of all of them.

It also made me think back to my own, "I wish" and "I'm not enough" moments.

Maybe I *was* enough.

Thank you, ladies of Oregon, for your unlimited tenacity.

Most of all, thank you for your ongoing support of one another in both your business and in raising your families.

You are enough!

* * *

*Take a moment to reflect and write down your thoughts. Note pages are available in the back of the book.*

CHAPTER 8

# Leadership vs. Management

J ust like my early days of motherhood, my early days of management were wrought with "I wish I would have done that better."

I wouldn't say I was a born leader. I am a doer. No matter the size of the job, I will work hard to complete it and do the best I can.

I once had a newer rep on my team call me a workhorse. I took that as a compliment since he owned a working farm and had worked with horses.

As aforementioned, I pursued management to escape a stressful time in my life. Moving to a new city with a fresh start seemed like the answer.

I am an achievement-oriented person. By the time I chose management as my next career path, I had achieved the goals I set for myself in my current role. I was looking for a new challenge.

I sure found one!

Walking into a leadership role with no training involves a lot of trial and error. At first, I thought, "I'm the boss!" That means everyone will just do as I say. Afterall, I was an exceptional sales rep.

Yeah, right....

I was too cocky, too confident, and too much of *all* the wrong things.

I believed work was the only real control I had in my life. Moving into a management role demolished that control. I would now have to rely on others to hit nearly any goal and objective I set.

Could I recruit the right people? Could I train them to be successful?

With the awareness of my newly decreased control came a new fear: what if I couldn't be a good manager? I could be fired! As a single mom, that was a catastrophic fear.

How long would they give me to turn this beast around? I was afraid to ask that question.

Like most people, fear can come out in negative ways. I was demanding. I was too fast paced in everything. I showed my frustration constantly.

I was managing the problems, but I wasn't leading. I was ineffective and quite frankly, blowing it in this new role.

With only one other woman on the team, who always looked like she had her shit together and knew exactly what to do, I didn't know where to turn. I just kept making the same mistakes, hiring the wrong people, making poor decisions, and scaring people away.

Thankfully, I hired a couple of effective employees who helped me become a better leader. They were people that didn't hesitate to discuss their issues with me and telling me what they needed from me, as their manager, to be successful.

I needed to stop telling them what to do and teach them.

I voiced my concerns to a dear friend who was a trainer with our company. He questioned how long it took for me to become successful in my last role with the company. My response was three to four years.

"Then what makes you feel you can be great at this so quickly?" he replied.

AHA!

Another AHA moment happened not long after this conversation. Our district leadership changed, and our new boss came to visit our office during his first couple months.

When he walked into my personal office and saw my awards from my previous role lining the walls, he congratulated me on my achievements. Then he said, "Maybe it's time to quit living on past successes and work on new ones as a leader."

My first thought was, JERK! But I realized he was right. All those awards said to my team was that I was better than them. They shouted, "SEE, if I can do it why can't you?!"

I was proud of my accomplishments during that part of my career, but that was over.

I needed to change my vision of success. It wasn't about me failing or succeeding, it was about the *team* succeeding. I took the awards down and put up a white board where I could write my vision for the team.

After these two AHA moments, I started to slow down so I could assess a situation with more clarity. I made sure I had time to consider goals for the next week, month, or year and then list the actions needed to obtain those results.

It took me three years to fine tune this process and meet 100% of our corporate objectives. Fine tune doesn't mean I perfected the process and success happened every year. Of my 30 years in field sales, I hit those corporate objectives 50% of the time. I would get on a streak five to six years in a row and then BOOM, back to the bottom.

Change is constant in leadership. Change can instigate the fight or flight mentality that can take a team from the top to the bottom quickly if not approached as a leader.

Managers manage change.

Leaders lead through change.

In the beginning of my management career, I approached change in defense mode. Constantly battling with my team, trying to prove I was the boss. I would defend the change, no matter how big or small. I was dismissive of their individual fears and of what this change meant to them. I just wanted my team to sell. I can honestly say this approach never made me feel good. It was exhausting. I just didn't know how to adjust my approach.

At one point, I lost more than 50% of my team.

Employee retention is key to success in any business. Having to continually recruit the right people and train them costs companies millions of dollars. Mine was not different.

I was failing. I needed to understand where I was failing.

I asked my supervisor to have human resources go back 18 months and perform exit interviews with every person I lost from my team. I was hoping for a common denominator—an answer. I needed to correct or reverse this poor retention trend.

My supervisor had obvious concerns about my retention but was still hesitant about this request.

"Are you sure you want this information in writing?" and "You're already on upper management's radar," were his responses.

The fear of losing my job was real. I was helping them gather information that could be used against me, but I needed that information to diagnose and fix the problems in my office.

I made the decision to go all in. What I discovered from their feedback was invaluable.

I learned where I could make the biggest changes to turn this trend around. It was ME! My response to change was the first piece. The next piece that needed work was improving our training systems for the new recruits. Stronger leadership skills motivate others to *want* to be on your team. I felt renewed direction, equipped with this information and what I had learned from it.

On the other hand, the results of obtaining that information came with harsh criticism from my superiors. One of them told me, "You better be the turnaround story of the year."

I could have turned those results and criticism into defeat. Instead, I decided I wanted to grow as a leader, whether it was with my current company or the next opportunity, if need be. I was determined to work on my leadership skills regardless of where they would be used.

I wasn't the "turnaround story of the year" but I didn't get fired either. I believe my superiors saw those fundamental changes I was making in both my leadership skills and my hiring and training processes.

With these changes, we became a successful team once again. We learned as a team how to navigate change. I became a better listener. I stopped forming answers in my head before a team member was done talking. I stopped holding my breath during conversations regarding change.

Rather than being defensive, I became understanding, and compassionate to how change affected my team. The tone of these conversations turned into "How can we use this change to grow their businesses?"

Together, we learned to diagnose and develop strategies to work through change.

Again, this was not perfected overnight.

Change is uncomfortable. It can be easier to slip back into your old way of doing things.

I have often used the analogy of new high heels vs. old fuzzy slippers. Those fuzzy slippers are comfy and fit your feet perfectly after wearing them for so many years. But those new high heels look amazing, you just have to break them in!

The difference was our shift in attitude towards change that brought the team back to the top. It allowed us to start brainstorming ways to grow. There was still frustration. There were still members of the team who were defensive.

Around this time, I became a company trainer for a

process called Periodization, by Brian Welsh. I fell in love with the process of developing shorter goals with daily tactics and accountability.

This take-charge process allowed us to correct our strategies quicker and redefine each person's definition of success.

I discovered that allowing each team member to decide what success meant to them gave them ownership in their goals so they could achieve that definition.

Rather than taking my assigned production goals and telling each person their share, I would take their goals for their business and help break it down.

I discovered their definition of success usually contributed to our team's success but in their own words.

Then, I helped them develop strategies to obtain their goals. This was way more fun than the constant, "you aren't doing your fair share" conversations of years past.

The "It's a 12-month contest" comments disappeared. The sense of urgency to reach these shorter goals was astonishing.

The theory is to breakdown your annual goal thinking into 12-week segments. Putting together strategies and daily tactics to reach these 12-week goals. At the end of the 12 weeks, you can see where your strategies worked or faltered rather than waiting until the end of a year to adapt your approach.

I won't take time to explain the process in further detail, but if you're interested, look for Periodization by Brian Welsh. This change was by far the most effective in turning me from a manager into a leader.

Some team members jumped into this quickly. Others took more time.

We had a senior team member who hated accountability. He had many successful years doing it his way and saw little reason to change. On his off years he was always on the defensive—he was someone who made me hold my breath during conversations.

He helped make me a better leader because he could be difficult. Smooth seas don't make a skilled sailor, as they say.

At the start of the transition, he hated the idea of giving me a definition of success. This would mean that he would give me a goal to help with that definition. That would mean he would be accountable. Yikes.

I think he finally got tired of me asking questions and wrote down his definition of success. We then discussed strategies and tactics to help reach that goal. We set a date to chat again in 12 weeks.

Because he had been on the team so long, he was used to the "your fair share" comments during our discussions. When I went to his office for his 12-week review, he was in total defense mode. I knew that he hadn't reached his goals, nor had he attempted to do any of the strategies or daily tactics we laid out.

When I walked into his office, he was sitting behind his desk with his arms crossed and a scowl on his face. He looked ready for a fight. I looked at him and said, "Bet you're glad that's over?"

"Glad what's over?" he scowled.

"Those 12 weeks! Now we can start fresh and figure out what you really want to do."

Not the conversation he was expecting! I realized that not everyone will grasp every aspect of such a huge change in thinking. Some need to take smaller steps. By allowing him to adapt without penalty, he started to see the value in this change.

Change is constant. Without change, there can be no growth in yourself or your business.

If learning how to process change was the key to my success, then finding ways to bring about change was turning the lock.

Change is growth!

Change is uncomfortable!

It's okay to be uncomfortable. The changes I made in my leadership skills were uncomfortable but necessary for my growth as a leader.

It's okay to be wrong. It's okay to make mistakes. That's how we learn. That's how we grow.

While the team grew and became increasingly successful, I never forgot the years we spent at the bottom were the years that taught me the most about leadership.

During these years of growth, our focus was internal. We were looking only at our business growth. I noticed we were still missing something.

We were known among our competitors as the company to watch. Community leaders and non-profits began reaching out, asking the team to become involved in various projects in our community.

We mostly declined these invitations, for a while. We were too busy with the momentum of success and internal growth, not to mention our family lives.

Reverting to my old ways, I forced everyone to join an industry organization that I had chosen to support. I saw value in this organization through their education and political support of our industry.

Old habits die hard.

My team had no real desire to belong to this group. It wasn't as important to them as it was to me. Those defensive conversations resurfaced again, and division crept back onto the team.

Ideas come at the strangest times and places....

Later that year, I was taking an early morning flight to a business conference. I am an early boarder; I like to find my space, get settled, and begin my journey. I am not the chatty person on flights. I make it a point to have a book or newspaper open to avoid conversation. Traveling for business was my only alone time with my thoughts, and it was common I'd think of new strategies or changes I wanted to work on during these trips.

This particular trip was at the end of a transitional year for our company. I was looking forward to visiting with my peers about their change processes and seeing old friends.

As I assumed my "don't talk to me" position the mayor of our fair city boarded the plane. When she got close to where I was sitting, she stopped in the aisle.

"Good morning, Nita! Congrats on your new location. The sign on the building looks amazing!"

Wait. What just happened? I didn't realize she knew I existed, let alone my name and the agency's recent move to a larger location. I may have spoken a few words back to her, but I don't remember. My wheels were spinning!

*Community.* That's what was missing.

We needed to be bigger than ourselves. We needed to look outside our business and see our community. Living in a college town, you assume that's all there is to the culture, but is it?

I didn't have that answer.

We spent the last 14 years becoming a well-known, recognizable team but did we know the heart of our community?

Most team members were involved in their church or their kids' sports team but what about the *team*? What were we doing as a fast-growing company to support the heart of our community?

Again, I didn't have the answer.

I began to draw up a strategy to meet with these community leaders to learn these answers.

Step 1: Allow team members to choose the community group they wanted to support. Why was I forcing them to belong to an organization that I believed in?

Step 2: Design a contest where the winner's prize goes to

the local nonprofit of their choice instead of their pocket (and forgotten ten minutes later).

Step 3: List people I wanted to meet and how I would get referrals.

Steps one and two were easy. Step three was going to be a struggle. Who did I know and why would they refer me?

I spent so much time growing a team and raising kids, I had no idea where to start.

But wait a minute, isn't that what my team members struggle with every day? How to get in front of people and how to get referrals?

As this fundamental change started to take shape, I realized I needed the help of the entire team. I needed to prove that I could get in front of people of influence in our community.

The "Heart of the Community" project was born.

I sat down with a couple of my consistent top producers and laid out my strategy. They loved the idea and contributed to the list of people we should meet.

They formed teams for the new contest and chose the nonprofit that would receive the top prize money.

Needless to say, they were elated to choose an organization to belong to rather than be forced into one.

In order for this change to take hold, I needed to be diligent to avoid reverting to my "manager" ways and stay on the path of a leader.

Before we could put the entire project into place, another change disrupted our plans. And, as is the nature of change, it came when least expected.

Change likes it that way. Your true character shows when change comes unexpectedly.

After 15 years in my current location building this team and becoming an empty nester, I was asked to move and take over another team that had some really great individual members but no synergy as a team.

Like most opportunities within our company, you don't have much time to make a decision.

You are only one chess piece in this game. Another move can't be made until you give your answer. I had a week.

Personally, this relocation was easier than the last time: I had my Happily Ever After to help with the decision, no kids at home, and no debt.

Professionally, I felt like I was abandoning a team that I had built.

I had one assistant the entire 15 years. She knew me better than my husband! I remember the pain of starting over with staffing. Did I want to do that again?

My assistant told me it was like we were getting divorced, and she was keeping all the kids. YIKES!

However, I love a new challenge and this one was too great to pass up.

This would be an opportunity to avoid past mistakes. I was excited to step into this position as an effective leader.

I had learned how to help my old team grow their business through a consultative approach. As one of the most senior teams in the district, I looked forward to helping my new team grow individually and as a team.

I spent the first two months meeting with each team member individually, asking questions about their business and meeting their staff. I did not review their sales production or their current ranking within the company.

I didn't want to have any preconceived ideas about their business based on corporate objectives. I, of course, knew who the top producers were. My choice to get to know them apart from their performance was different than their previous leadership.

I had known many of these people most of my career— some from corporate conferences I had attended as a sales rep so many years ago.

This team was comfortable right where they were in their businesses. They were comfortable not being a team.

My favorite phone call from those first weeks was to a team member I considered a good friend. When I called his office, his assistant (and also his wife) told me he wasn't available. I pushed a little to find out when he would be available, and she gave me his cell number. He was fishing that day.

I was really looking forward to chatting with him, so I decided to give him a call right away. I didn't mind that he was out fishing; good for him!

When he heard my voice, he immediately launched into a ten-minute tirade about his business. He knew all his clients. His book of business was completely tapped out—no growth potential. The company expectations were not his expectations and on and on.

When he finally took a breath, I replied, "Wow! I was just calling to say how excited I am that we are finally going to get to work together."

We shared a good laugh over this conversation for many years.

Once I had met with each person individually, I set our first all-agency team meeting. During this meeting I discussed what they could expect from me and how my approach to their business would be diagnostic. I let them know I would always come to them with not only growth strategies, but with actual tactics they or their staff could immediately implement.

I felt my job was to be their personal business consultant and my primary objective was to help them grow. I also planned to help them better manage their business and increase efficiency.

One of the senior members raised his hand. He thanked me for taking the time to learn about each person's business individually, and he was glad to know what to expect from me, but he had a question:

"What do *you* expect from *us*?"

Without hesitation I replied, "I expect you to be uncomfortable again."

Change is uncomfortable, but change is growth. Time to put away those comfy slippers and break in those amazing new high heels.

My time with this team was the most fun I've had in my career. I kept my promise to help them grow (or with some of them to move on to the next chapter of their lives). It wasn't perfect by any means. The mistakes I made early in my management career taught me how to be more effective as a leader. My leadership showed very quickly: this team became a top team in the company within the first year of my leadership.

Moving to a new city, I was eager to start my "Heart of the Community" project, but I didn't know where to start. I didn't want to rely on my new team members for referrals. I hadn't proven myself yet and felt I needed to earn their referrals.

My new community was in the same state as my previous, only 50 miles away.

I had two women in my previous network who served as consultants across the state. I set up lunch with them both and laid out the Heart of the Community project.

They each gave me one referral. Those two referrals grew very quickly into a large network of local community businesses and nonprofit leaders.

I was fortunate that our company had an established presence in my new community. We already had a reputation of giving.

The best advice I received at the beginning of building my network was to attend every business and nonprofit event for one full year. At the end of that year, I would know the heart of the community and where I could be of the most help.

I enjoyed this project immensely. I met many wonderful

people. They taught me innumerable lessons about civic responsibility.

Born from an interaction on an early-morning flight, this project was making a difference within the community and the business.

It was a great lesson in looking beyond our own everyday struggles as leaders and business owners. I only wish I had time to implement Heart of the Community with my previous team. I believe it was the missing piece.

Success comes from making mistakes. It also comes from not giving up because of those mistakes.

I will be forever grateful to have worked with a company that continually pushed me to become a better leader and a better person. Success for me was just on the other side of fear.

*Take a moment to reflect and write down your thoughts. Note pages are available in the back of the book.*

# CHAPTER 9

## Hope

There have been many dark days in my life. However, HOPE allows the bright days to outnumber the dark days.

During those dark days, I would pray that time would go by quickly so I could get to the other side—so I could look back on that time rather than be in it.

Hope and Prayer are my saviors.

Hope and Prayer are my constants.

No matter how dark the day, I know in my heart there is a light at the end of the darkness. Sometimes, it is barely a pinprick of light, but I know it is always there. I believed I would come out the other side and be wearing sunglasses in the brightness of that light.

My mother always said everything was temporary, the good and the bad. That's a great thought during bad times but can be ominous during good times. Nonetheless, I kept the "this is only temporary" mantra in my head during the most challenging times in my life.

I originally submitted the manuscript for this book without the last chapter. I had already named it HOPE, but I wanted to take my time to get it just right—to end this story with a bang that would stay with the reader. I prayed to God to help me find the words to empower other women as they walked through their tough times as professionals and mothers.

Less than a month after I submitted the manuscript, I was told that I had endometrial cancer.

Well, that's one way to help! Test my strength. Test my faith. Test my ability to hold on to hope.

But strong I remain. Strong for my family. Their fear is worse to me than what I am going through. I wanted to wait until after surgery and the "all clear" before telling my children. They have busy lives, and I didn't want to worry them.

How typical of all strong professional women? Protect our children and those we care about from anything that may hurt them or cause them to worry. Protect them from our dark days.

My Hubby and I decided to tell them prior to surgery. You know what? We raised some strong adult humans! They are supportive, not only of me, but of each other. They are capable of facing this head on and come together. I believe they have spoken to each other more in the past month than in the past year. They know how to support each other in a crisis.

My faith remains strong. I have moments of fear for what this diagnosis brings. I remind myself, "Don't let fear of tomorrow take away from the joys of today!" I am, once again working hard to stay in the moment and not let my mind wander to what ifs.

HOPE, knowing there is light at the end of this tunnel, is in my heart.

Gratitude for a life well-lived eliminates the fears of tomorrow.

Facing this new challenge reminds me of other challenges I have faced. In our minds, the current crisis always seems like the worst of all crises we have endured. In the past when those dark times would come, I would go back to old journals I have kept reliving how I emerged from that crisis.

Have I mentioned journaling?

I have no doubt that writing down my deepest and truest feelings and thoughts saved me many times. I'm also sure this outlet saved other people in my life from getting the wrath of my stress.

I received my first diary when I was in fourth grade. Some of you will remember your own little blue book with "Diary" written in gold across the front. It came with a lock and key to hold your secrets. I fell in love with writing the day I received this gift. I, like most girls, didn't write every day but when there was drama, it went in that little book.

Years later, when one of my daughters was the typical, struggling fourth grader, I showed her my diary from when I was her age. I wanted her to see that everything she was feeling was normal and she would be just fine.

She took my treasured first diary into her room and spent a couple hours reading my deepest thoughts as a ten-year-old. I worried a little, trying to remember what I had written all those years ago. The best I could do is remember this mean girl who pushed me out of the back of a truck and breaking my arm as a result.

When she returned the diary to me later that day, she seemed lighter and more confident. Just as I was congratulating myself on a great motherhood decision to share my heart with her, she said, "Boy Mom, you were messed up as a kid."

And off she went. Not exactly the reaction I was expecting but she felt better about herself.

I became one of those people who kept two journals every year: one for business and one personal. I kept them in separate locations, because just like my life, I kept these two parts away from each other as much as possible.

As you can imagine, I had quite a collection by the time I

was getting ready to retire. I made the decision to clean them out. I didn't need to take the whole collection with me. Further, I don't want my kids reading those "dark day" entries someday. And who would want to read my business journals —boring!

Throwing out my business journals was easy. I had fun breezing through journals from years that saw huge changes in my career, either my location or my thinking on leadership. I enjoyed looking back on the crossroads that were instrumental changes for me and my family. Knowing how it all turned out made for a fun afternoon.

Then, I thought I should get rid of some of my personal journals. It was time to do a good, old-fashioned clean out.

While the covers of my business journals all looked the same, my personal journals were an array of colors or motivational covers. Just looking at the cover could bring back that year in my mind's eye. Just like my fourth-grade self I would make small entries about good stuff and spew pages during a crisis.

One journal burned my fingers the moment I touched it.

The cover was colored blocks with shadows of cats in each block. I remember liking the design when I bought it. The year inside held some of my darkest days in my adult life.

I took the journal, holding it away from me with two fingers and took it to the recycling bin. This one deserved its very own burial. I tossed it in and walked away.

Nothing good in there to review! See ya!

I went back into the house to continue the big clean out.

About ten minutes later, I started to panic. What if someone at the recycling facility took it out and read it?!

Yeah, that's how irrational I got about it. A person at the recycling facility? Really!? But the panic was real. I went out to the recycle bin to retrieve the dreaded journal. This wasn't a small recycle bin—we were preparing to move, so we'd called in the big guns. I had just started the big clean out, so the bin was practically empty. Was I really going to go in headfirst to retrieve it? I guess I could tip it over and crawl in....

I attempted to calm myself and leave it there but that didn't last. I crawled in and pulled the journal out. "I know, I'll tear it up!" was my next thought. That way, the recycle guy would only see a page or two.

Even *I* am rolling my eyes at the irrational thoughts and fears of someone looking at the worst time I can remember.

As I opened the journal to start tearing the pages, my eyes fell on a January entry:

Be Brave

Be Fierce

Be Intentional

There it was, HOPE. Even in my darkest times.

I still shredded the journal, but later that day, I wrote a message of HOPE in my current journal.

The journal that held my thoughts and fears about retirement.

Retirement doesn't qualify as a dark time—just an unknown. We had worked hard for years to make sure we would be okay financially, but what about my busy mind?

What would I do with all that time on my hands? I spent my adult life raising kids and growing in my career. For Pete's sake, I didn't even have a hobby!!

Seeing that message of hope centered me in my thoughts. I let go of expectations of what I was going to do with the rest of my life. I had to intentionally refrain from projecting so far into the future and stay focused on the last few months of my career. My focus was to try to impact as many people as I could before I left.

You know what happened? The fear of this huge life change went away. I went back to living in the present.

My hubby, who retired at 40 to be the stay-at-home parent to our youngest three was full of advice. "Give yourself six months to get used to it." He would constantly ask how I was doing as my retirement approached. My response was always, "I have no expectations."

What a gift that message of Hope from so long ago has been the last 15 months.

Hope is just that, a gift. A gift you can give yourself and others.

When you share the gift of Hope you give someone the power to be brave, be fierce, and to act intentionally.

Hope can take away the fear of tomorrow.

This new challenge will become an experience that will become part of who I am.

God has my back now, just like He has my whole life. HOPE is His way of showing me my story is just beginning.

* * *

*Take a moment to reflect and write down your thoughts. Note pages are available in the back of the book.*

CHAPTER 10

# *Reflections*

I t is my hope that as you Walk With Me through my journey that you will take time to write down reflections on your journey.

Reflections can serve a dual purpose.

First, as a reminder of the challenges you have faced and lessons you learned along the way. These are good reminders during those times when you want to throw your hands in the air or stomp your feet. YOU have made it through worse and came out stronger!

Second, as a path for your future. Write down those BIG dreams. Start the process of outlining a strategy. As I have heard my entire professional life, "Goals are just dreams until you write them down."

Above all else, YOU ARE ENOUGH!

# PART ONE

*Journaling Pages*

# 1
## TENACITY

- Have you had your snowdrift in the hallway/AHA moment? Did you recognize it as an AHA moment?
- When you think about the personality trait that you are most proud of, do you realize it was born out of hardship?

## 2
## CHOICES

- How do you move through periods of change?
- Is this process different for your personal life vs. your professional life?

# 3
# PATIENCE

- Do you have a process to write out a strategy for your long- and short-term goals?
- Who is in your tribe? What do they bring to the team? What do you bring to them?

Patience is time! Time needs a strategy!

# 4
## INNER STRENGTH

- Do people in your life see you as the calm flight attendant? Do your children?
- Describe your inner strength. How do you continue to develop this strength?

_____

_____

_____

_____

_____

_____

_____

_____

_____

_____

_____

_____

_____

_____

_____

_____

# HUMOR

- Have you been the brunt of humor? How do you use humor?
- When was the last time you had a true belly laugh?

_____
_____
_____
_____
_____
_____
_____
_____
_____
_____
_____
_____
_____
_____
_____
_____
_____
_____
_____

# 6
## PERCEPTION OF PERFECTION

- Do you have a BIG Dream? What is your timeline to achieve this BIG Dream?
- Who are the people, places, and things you need to achieve this BIG Dream?

# MOTHERHOOD (VS. CHILDBIRTH)

- How do you balance your personal and professional life? Does your tribe play a part in this balance?
- Describe a situation when you were fully present with your children. These are great reminders that, YOU ARE ENOUGH.

# LEADERSHIP VS. MANAGEMENT

- Do you have a time in your professional life when YOU were the biggest change needed? Consider your attitude or your approach to people or situations.
- Describe a time when you were brave enough to change YOU.
- Implementation can be the hardest part of change; how do you manage this process?

## HOPE

- What does HOPE mean to you? How do you see it in your life as a professional who is also a mom?
- Have you had a situation in your personal or professional life where you definitely weren't as brave as your face appeared?

# About the Author

Nita Kennedy is an author, consultant, and retired corporate leader, who now bridges her writing and love of photography through her passion initiative of "Walk with Me." It's her mission to empower people through sharing her experience, strength, and hope. She currently lives in Lake Havasu City, AZ with her Happily Ever After and her beautiful mama, where her love of desert and water come together. She also enjoys traveling throughout the United States discovering the beauty of her country.

To connect with Nita and learn more, visit her website at:
www.NitaKennedy.com

 facebook.com/nita.kennedy.3
linkedin.com/in/anita-kennedy-b805702

# Praise for Nita Kennedy

*Nita brings strategic thought, diligent success planning techniques, an empathetic spirit and creative business solutions in her consultative practice. I have watched Nita positively impact individuals careers for decades. She makes a difference for everyone she works with by listening to their needs, goals and desires. She helps build a plan of accountability that will lead you to improved results. You need Nita on your professional team!*

Tim Harris, Executive Vice President of Agency Operations, COUNTRY Financial

\* \* \*

*Nita Kennedy is the real deal. Together we co-piloted Family Building Blocks for two years, me as ED and she as Board Chair. Wise, patient, and very funny, Nita navigated every opportunity and challenge expertly. Constantly by my side, she helped me sort through everything that an ED faces, helped me prioritize, and provided timely reality checks. Best of all, she never let me take myself too seriously and always made me laugh!*

Patrice Altenhofen, Executive Director of Family Building Blocks

\* \* \*

## CONTINUED PRAISE

*Anita has been a caring, energetic, and strategic community partner for our non-profit. She forms outcome-based partnerships and is someone who gets things done. Anita influences positive change in communities and causes she cares about. She pushes me to grow as a nonprofit leader and I consider her not just a mentor, but also a friend.*

Jerry Ambris, Executive Director of Habitat for Humanity, Mid-Williamette Valley

* * *

*Anita is an experienced leader with a proven track record of motivating and supporting women. Her significant accomplishment in creating leaders fuels her desire to coach women to reach their full potential by rediscovering their purpose and become the best version of themselves.*

Bonnie Milletto, Empowerment Speaker & Author

* * *

*Nita Kennedy has been an exceptional mentor to me and to so many. She has a way of providing a perfect balance of empathy and empowerment while challenging and problem-solving. I would say she introduced 'tough love' to me as a leader. Her willingness to share her own experiences and wisdom while listening closely are qualities that many of her mentees have learned from. She has engrained confidence into the women in her circle; both professionally and personally. Her unrelenting determination paved the way and honestly pushed the many excuses out the window of female business owners. Respect is earned, not given and Nita has earned it across the board. Nita shared life-changing lessons with me, and they have truly shaped my career. She reminds women of what's most important in life. She motivates without being expected or asked to. The trust she earned in our business came from the unending support she provided to all. She could relate and that provided empathy, but it also provided solutions. Nita always found time and made you feel that you were her top priority. Her high expectations come from the passion to push others to their true potential. I can never thank her enough for what she saw in me and the perfect mix of motivation, assurance, and tough love.*

Kendall Holmes
Vice President of Operations, COUNTRY Financial

\* \* \*

CPSIA information can be obtained
at www.ICGtesting.com
Printed in the USA
BVHW030254041222
653406BV00008B/26/J